When His
SECRET
SIN
Breaks Your

heart

Letters to
Hurting Wives

KATHY
GALLAGHER

Foreword by
BEVERLY LaHAYE

ALSO AVAILABLE BY PURE LIFE MINISTRIES:

At the Altar of Sexual Idolatry
A Biblical Guide to Counseling the Sexual Addict
Create in Me a Pure Heart
From Ashes to Beauty
He Leads Me Beside Still Waters
How America Lost Her Innocence
Intoxicated with Babylon
Irresistible to God
A Lamp Unto My Feet
Living in Victory
Out of the Depths of Sexual Sin
Pressing On Toward the Heavenly Calling
Standing Firm Through the Great Apostasy
The Walk of Repentance

For these books and other teaching materials please contact:

PURE LIFE MINISTRIES
14 School Street
Dry Ridge, KY 41035
(888) PURELIFE - to order
(859) 824-4444
(859) 813-0005 FAX
www.purelifeministries.org

Acknowledgments

I was told by a friend before I began writing these letters that it would be very difficult and heavy, but that it was God's will. I have found that statement to be true.

I want first of all to thank the Lord for all of His mercy and severity. He has been patient and compassionate with me, and yet He has been unrelenting in His desire to make me live the words I've written in this book. I will love Him forever for caring enough about me not to spoil me.

I want to thank Rosaline Bush for being the catalyst God used to get me started on this project. "How delightful is a word spoken in due season."

I want to thank my husband for his encouragement not to give up, and for the countless hours he spent editing and rewriting.

I want to thank my dear friend and comrade in the faith, Rose Colón, who has been so faithful to go down into the trenches, to help bear the weight of so many broken hearts.

I also want to thank Ken and Robin Halcomb and Bradley Furges for their diligent help in editing.

And lastly, Wayne Brown, the one counselor who had the courage to confront Steve Gallagher, many years ago. Thank you, Wayne, for your help editing, also.

Dedication

This book is dedicated to my beloved.
How far we have come, from ashes to beauty.
The Lord has made our crooked paths straight,
and you have become to me the love of God personified.
Thank you for loving me and being faithful to me.
Truly my beloved is mine, and I am his.

TABLE OF CONTENTS

Foreword — 9

Introduction — 11

My Story — 15

HIS PRESENCE THROUGH PAIN — *Dear Melody* — 26
THE HUSBAND'S STRUGGLE — *Dear Miriam* — 29
DEALING WITH SUSPICIONS — *Dear Janet* — 32
WHY SHOULD I PUT UP WITH THIS? — *Dear Lauren* — 35
THE ENCOURAGING WIFE — *Dear Ann* — 39
THE ANGRY WIFE — *Dear Deborah* — 41
I FEEL LIKE I'M LOSING MY MIND! — *Dear Anna* — 43
JUST STOP IT! — *Dear Janie* — 45
CONDEMNATION AND WORSHIP — *Dear Karen* — 47
THE WRONG OBSESSION — *Dear Bernice* — 50
TOO MANY VOICES — *Dear Cynthia* — 51
FILLING THE VOID — *Dear Susan* — 52
THE TV BATTLE — *Dear Patricia* — 54
FRUITS OF REPENTANCE — *Dear Pam* — 55
CONFRONTING THE HUSBAND — *Dear Joyce* — 58
THE ABUSIVE HUSBAND — *Dear Elaine* — 60
WHERE IS GOD? — *Dear Jenny* — 62
VAGUE SUSPICIONS — *Dear Laura* — 64
FEAR OF OTHER WOMEN — *Dear Rachel* — 66
ABANDONED BY GOD — *Dear Shirley* — 68
BEARING THE BURDEN — *Dear Clara* — 70
THE ROOTS OF HOMOSEXUALITY — *Dear Janice* — 72
THE APPEASING WIFE — *Dear Judy* — 74
INTERCESSION FOR THE HUSBAND — *Dear Terry* — 77
A FATHER'S CHASTISEMENT — *Dear Lucy* — 81

Marriage In a Rut — *Dear Connie*   83

Dealing With Fear — *Dear Alice*   86

The Failing Husband — *Dear Veronica*   89

The Neglected Wife — *Dear Tammy*   91

The Police Wife — *Dear Kelly*   94

Reconciliation — *Dear Sonja*   96

The Aggravated Wife — *Dear Penny*   99

The Love Life — *Dear Paula*   101

The Relentless Wife — *Dear Margaret*   104

The Unrepentant Husband — *Dear Sue*   107

The Adulteress Wife — *Dear Stacey*   109

My Sexual Needs — *Dear Darlene*   111

The Child Molester — *Dear Ericka*   115

Accountability — *Dear Deanna*   119

Divorce — *Dear Theresa*   123

Lost Respect — *Dear Jeri*   125

The Mercy Life — *Dear Yolanda*   127

Lost Love — *Dear Diane*   129

Untrustworthy With Money — *Dear Carla*   133

High Expectations — *Dear Gloria*   135

Watching Pornography — *Dear Wanda*   138

The Importance of Gratitude — *Dear Sylvia*   140

Don't Stop Believing — *Dear Marcie*   143

The Enabler Wife — *Dear Robin*   144

Separated With A Boyfriend — *Dear Lisa*   146

Letter From A Husband — *Dear Valerie*   148

Dealing With Unforgiveness — *Dear Rita*   150

Feeling Betrayed — *Dear Rebecca*   152

Bizarre Sex — *Dear Elizabeth*   154

Fairy-Tale Marriage — *Dear Heather*   156

Engaged to a Porn Addict — *Dear Alissa*   158

Journal   159

$\mathcal{W}$e see them every day as we go through life's daily routine. Sexual images constantly bombard us—in newspapers, magazines, movies, billboards, television. And now they can be easily accessed through the Internet. Add to this that pornography, homosexuality and adulterous affairs have become not only prevalent but acceptable, and we now have a society that has become saturated with sex.

Therefore, it comes as no surprise that many men have found it difficult to keep their minds pure and have succumbed to some type of sexual sin. Pornography is the most common form of sexual sin, and it is estimated that 40 percent of American men purchase erotic materials each year. Adult entertainment is a multi-billion dollar industry, and those who profit from it know that the addictive nature of pornography and related activities lead men to spend an increasing amount of money and energy in pursuit of them. But what many fail to realize is that sexual sin carries with it a greater cost than the impact on a man's wallet. It can devastate all of his relationships—especially with his wife and children.

The church is now beginning to recognize that pornography and prostitution are also problems for Christian men. In the past these problems were either ignored or thought to be limited to those men outside the church. Thankfully, many pastors and congregations are starting to deal with what has been called the church's "secret sin" and are providing Bible studies and support groups for men and women affected by sexual sin.

If you are a wife whose husband is involved in sexual sin, my heart goes out to you! This is one of the deepest betrayals that a woman faces. Often times you may feel alone, afraid, frustrated, and unsure of where to turn for help. I want you to know that you are not alone. God has been watching over you, and He will continue to do so. He wants to be your source of strength. It is not an easy road to travel, but God has promised that he will provide you with the strength you need to endure. And in the midst of these trying times, you will develop a deeper relationship with God if you rely on Him. He is both loving and faithful. At the same time, God may use these circumstances to smooth some rough edges and to develop character within you.

This book is also written for friends and family members who know women whose husbands have strayed sexually. You will develop a greater understanding of the struggles these wives face. They need encouragement, support, confidentiality, prayer and Biblical counseling. The Apostle Paul admonished believers to bear one another's burdens. This is a difficult burden for a woman to bear alone, and Satan can easily lead her into despair, anger, and bitterness. Your love and support for her can make a difference in not only her life but also the life of her husband as she strives to help him.

When a wife finds out that her husband is involved in a sexual sin, many emotions and questions run through her mind. Kathy's personal experience and her years of counseling wives have provided her with tremendous insight into the doubts and uncertainties they face.

Beverly LaHaye
Concerned Women for America

*I*n today's decadent society there are many diverse combinations of marital problems which may arise when a spouse is controlled by some life-dominating sin. This book is a compilation of letters written to hurting wives whose husbands have been in or are presently involved in sexual sin. I have chosen specific letters that address the common denominators these wives face such as: lack of trust, fear, hopelessness, doubt, anger, unforgiveness, and so forth. You will find each letter to be very supportive, offering much hope and encouragement. You may even discover that you are not alone—that finally there is someone who really understands your situation. What's more, this book offers hurting wives godly counsel and practical advice—some of which goes against the grain of many of the popular "solutions" marketed these days.

That brings me to another important point. As you read these letters you will find some that seem to encourage you along a path you have been taking that isn't right. Let me explain. Perhaps you have already determined to divorce your husband even though his problems have not been any worse than occasionally viewing pornography. If you already have this tendency, then you don't want to read the letter written to Samantha, where I actually encouraged her to leave her husband. Her situation warrants it. Yours wouldn't. But, if you were determined only to read what you want to read, then you could use those words in an attempt to justify your actions. I would suggest, instead, that you read the letters to Theresa and Lauren.

Perhaps you are weak, beaten down and would rather forget that you just discovered your husband is in adultery. You need the encouragement to be strong for your husband, as outlined in the letters to Judy and Robin. You wouldn't want to follow the advice found in the letter to Kelly who wants to police every move of her husband.

Another matter of importance that needs to be addressed, is that these letters of advice were written from a completely biblical perspective. God's design of handling offenses isn't always the easiest path to take. Indeed, you can go into almost any Christian bookstore in the country and find many books which, in the name of Christian love, give an alternative to those answers found in Scripture. I cannot answer for these authors. All I can say is that the Lord has not given me the liberty to give counsel outside of the parameters He has set forth in His Word.

My experience has been that those who gravitate toward the easier solutions and prefer pat answers offered by popular psychology over biblical solutions usually suffer most in the end. Dealing with life's problems God's way may often seem difficult, but those who choose to do so always reap the benefits in the end. A new person emerges, not because of any self-esteem revival, but as a result of having found the presence of the Lord to be sufficient through every trial and every struggle.

In some ways, I had my own struggles writing along these lines, knowing that, at times, it might seem to the reader, the broken one, that I lack compassion for her. There are instances in which I confront a wife in a letter that the reader might even think that I am, in some way, defending the sinful behavior of her husband. Please understand that my heart is for hurting wives because I too have experienced the same sorts of pain and despair myself. It is from much experience that I have come to the conviction that doing things God's way will always be richly rewarded. I refuse to succumb to pressure (i.e. compromise) or join the ranks of those who freely give women the easy way out. To do so would only amount to dispersing humanistic mercy rather than God's mercy which is always coupled with truth that sets us free. Narrow is the path that leads to life, and the ever-flowing life from God is exactly what hurting wives need most of all.

The purpose of this book is to provide the hurting wife with solid, biblical answers and practical solutions to everyday problems associated with being married to a man in sexual sin. Some of the more practical answers can, and should be, applied to life immediately. Others tend to be principles for living that are more idealistic and will only be attained through much effort and struggle. Remember that God is not an angry Judge, demanding perfection before He will hear your cry. Rather, He is a loving Father who wishes to help you through your painful trials. To Him, the greatest thing to come out of your situation is a deeper relationship with Himself. It is my hope that this book will lead you in that direction.

Kathy Gallagher

*I*n January of 1979 after several years of physical abuse, being married to a prospect of the Hells Angels, the interest in another man was the farthest thing from my mind. I finally felt free—free from the tyranny of a controlling husband, free from the fear in which I had constantly lived, and free from the abuse. I had a job, my own car, and most importantly, my own life.

But a few months prior to this, I had to flee for my life when I left my husband. He was a ruthless man and I was terrified of him. I remained incognito until things had calmed down with him enough so that I could resume my friendship with his older brother, Gale, and his wife, Joanne.

It was at their home in Sacramento one day that I first met Steve Gallagher. I was warming myself by the heater when he came waltzing through the front door of their little shack. My first impression of him was that he seemed out of place in that environment. Steve was a real estate agent and had come to Gale's house because he was interested in buying a home. Steve and Gale had done drugs and crime together in their earlier years but had not kept in touch with each other.

It never crossed my mind that I would some day become involved with this man. He was twenty-four, and I was only eighteen. He seemed so old to me. At any rate, as I began running into him at their house over the next few weeks, he began to pursue an interest in me. Steve later told me that, from the first time we met, he knew we were meant for each other. I didn't share this feeling and really had no desire to go out with him. Nevertheless, at Gale and Joanne's insistence, I finally agreed to a date.

He picked me up in his spacious Ford LTD and whisked me off to a drive-in movie. Before we had even gotten to the movie, he expressed his desire that I sit next to him. I informed him right off the bat that I felt no obligation to cuddle up beside a perfect stranger. So, our first date ended in an argument, with me angrily storming out of his car when he finally took me home. He yelled for me to come back, which I did, and after he humbled himself, and politely suggested we start all over again, I reluctantly agreed.

We continued to go out together over the next few weeks. One day he asked me to go with him to a beachside resort in Santa Cruz for a weekend—just the two of us. I knew what that meant: we would be in the same hotel room together for an entire weekend. This was heavy-duty. To me, it meant commitment; it meant that I was giving myself to him—I had to drop my guard and give my heart to him. I was very uneasy and unsure that I was ready to take the plunge. I think I even asked him, "Will we stay in the same room together?" I just wanted to make sure we understood each other.

This was a huge decision for me, one of the biggest of my adult life. In my mind, consenting to go was the same as saying "yes" to a marriage proposal. If I gave myself to him, it meant that I was his and he was mine. This wasn't just a date or a fun weekend with some guy that I liked. I had never done anything like this with anyone. Yet, in some way, I felt as though I was being pulled helplessly into this relationship which I couldn't resist. I finally agreed.

We were both full of excitement and had an absolutely wonderful time. You guessed it: I had fallen in love with "Prince Charming." Actually, I think I had loved Steve long before that weekend, but it was in Santa Cruz that I knew for sure I wanted to spend the rest of my life with him.

When we returned home on Sunday, we immediately moved in together. I was on cloud nine at first, but soon I began to see what Steve was really like. Full of ambition, he worked night and day in real estate. He was bent on becoming successful, but because of his great expectations he put undue pressure upon himself. This resulted in his short temper at home. I attributed his impatience with me to the stress of his real estate business and hoped that he would change eventually.

Despite all of this, a very interesting thing began to happen between us: Steve started to talk to me about God. He shared with me that he had first come to the Lord when he was doing jail time as a sixteen year-old but had backslidden shortly thereafter. He said that one day he wanted to get right with God again.

This was all news to me, but I immediately came under conviction because we had been living in sin together. Over the next few months, I lived with a sense of condemnation–that I was in trouble with God. But I didn't really know what to do about it.

Then, one day, I met Brother Jess at my sister's house. He was a sweet, Southern Baptist pastor who told me that I was a sinner in need of a Savior. The Lord had thoroughly prepared me for this divine appointment, and I made Jesus the Lord and Master of my life that day. The next day, I packed up all my belongings and left Steve.

Well, I fell in love with the Lord. I was on fire for Jesus. He became the center of my life. I spent hours reading the Word, awestruck by its profound wisdom and revelation of future events. I was in church whenever the doors opened and almost single-handedly turned that little church upside-down, infecting everyone with my newfound joy. Everywhere I went I talked to others about God. People couldn't believe the change that had come over me—I was a different person.

One day, zealous to see people come to know the Lord, I called Steve to try to witness to him. I wanted him to have what I had, but the years of being backslidden had made him hard-hearted toward God. When I had left him "for the Lord," he felt betrayed by God. At the end of our conversation, completely out of the blue, he told me to pray about whether we should be married. This was unthinkable! He was dead to spiritual realities, while I was completely happy serving God as a single Christian. Nevertheless, his words kept ringing in my ears over the next couple of weeks. I couldn't seem to escape them.

A month later, in January 1980, we were married. I had been a Christian for about five months. At first, he began attending church with me. Little by little though, he drifted away from God, once again, unwilling to surrender to the Lord.

Even though Steve was far more refined than my first husband, he was more difficult to live with. He never physically abused me, but I feared him more than my ex-husband who as I mentioned before was very abusive. Steve had a seething, violent anger that was always contained just under the surface. I saw him as the sort of person who could snap and just start killing people at random.

His anger—always directed at me—came through his sharp, cutting tongue. He was extremely critical and sarcastic. He would ridicule me whenever I did things wrong. I could never seem to satisfy him or do anything right. This, of course, left deep, emotional wounds that hurt far more than my first husband's fists.

Nevertheless, I tried to hope for the best. I knew that much of his frustration was due in part to the fact that the real estate market had suffered a tremendous blow with escalating interest rates. As a result Steve's career, which he had worked so hard to establish, began to crumble. No longer able to continue in real estate, he began looking for job opportunities in law enforcement.

This took us to Los Angeles where Steve began the long, excruciating process to become a deputy sheriff. Instead of things getting better, the stress of being on the Department made things even worse. He became even more abusive to me. Unfortunately, I sought Steve's approval, rather than God's. I became weaker and more dependent on him. Gradually, I too backslid. I would make feeble attempts to read my Bible and pray, but I had no strength or hunger inside. I had long since quit going to church.

Not long after we moved to Los Angeles, I found out about his addiction to pornography. According to Steve, it made him enjoy sex more. He gently let me know that I wasn't enough, but if we introduced porn into our marriage bed, he would be satisfied. Needless to say I was crushed. I had to compete with women in the pornographic movies and magazines. This was devastating to me, but instead of turning to God, I tried even harder to please Steve.

I intensely pursued his affection and love more than ever. I would have days when I felt like my heart would literally burst from the pain and rejection I felt. Other days, usually when he was sweet to me, I held out hope that he would change. I had decided to allow the pornography into our lives when he had assured me that it would only enhance our sex lives and make things better between us.

What happened, instead, was that the porn only drove him to demand more. To keep up with his insatiable appetite for sex, we eventually began getting sexually involved with other people. The only way I could handle the complete loss of my own dignity and self-respect was to drown them in drugs and alcohol. I became addicted to methamphetamine.

After several years of doing everything I could to win Steve, I finally gave up. I had loved him so much and had been willing to do literally anything to keep him, but his obsession with illicit sex had become insane. Having lost all hope, I left him and filed for divorce. I was devastated. Not only had I lost the battle to win him, but I had completely given up all my morals and self-respect in the meantime. I had to face what I had become.

It was then, almost like a miracle from God, that I met a guy named Tim. After years of emotional abuse, he was like a breath of fresh air! Immediately I forgot all the pain. Being with him helped me to stick my head in the sand and forget the loss I had suffered.

Tim was so good to me. He opened car doors for me, treated me with kindness and respect, and made me laugh a lot. Unlike Steve, he was very sensitive and considerate. Another thing I really appreciated was the way he would open up to me. This never happened with either of my husbands.

My involvement with Tim lasted for several weeks. Almost immediately I began sleeping with him, deceiving myself into believing that God would understand, because we really loved each other. His continuous drinking and quick willingness to be in adultery should have caused me to doubt his sincerity as a Christian, but I was so enthralled with him that I stifled my nagging doubts.

I had no contact with Steve during this time, so I didn't know that when I left he had gone back to his old ways of chasing girls. One morning, unbeknownst to me, he woke up in the apartment of one of his girl friends, feeling the emptiness of his life. All that day he was miserable. That afternoon he went to work at the jail, but it was a busy evening, so he didn't get back to eat his supper in the deputy chow hall until late. There were no other deputies there when he finally arrived. As he sat there, eating in miserable silence, a deputy named Willy strolled in. He, too, was late arriving and somehow the conversation got around to Steve's struggles. Upon hearing that Willy was a Christian, he poured out his heart to him, telling him how empty and unhappy he felt in life. Willy suggested that Steve give his heart to the Lord, which he did.

"I felt like a thousand pounds lifted off my back!" Steve exclaims. "But it didn't last long. When I got home that night, all I could think about was getting my wife back. I tossed and turned all night, upset about Kathy. In the middle of the night I heard a voice tell me that she would call in the morning. I didn't know if I was hearing things or what!"

The very next morning I had taken Tim to work, but after I dropped him off, I did a very strange thing: I started driving north on the freeway toward the San Fernando Valley where Steve and I had lived. I had no idea why I was doing this; it seemed like someone else was steering the car. When I got to Van Nuys, I stopped at a phone booth and called Steve.

He was very excited to hear from me, telling me what had happened the night before. I was glad to hear of his new life, but I had no intention of going back to him. My feelings for him were dead. I now had what I had wanted for so long. I was convinced that God had brought Tim into my life and I had no desire to go back to Steve. As far as I was concerned, he had lost his opportunity and now the Lord was restoring to me "all the years that the locust had eaten." By this time I was becoming accustomed to being treated like a princess. Tim was giving me the love that I had wanted from Steve; I would be a fool to return to him.

Finally, in desperation, Steve challenged me to call my parents for their advice. This I was more than happy to do, knowing how furious they had become with him when I told them all that he had been doing. I agreed and called them. My dad answered the phone, and when I explained the situation, to my surprise, he told me that the Lord had spoken to them about me, and clearly told them that I should return to my husband. I just sat down in the phone booth and cried. I didn't want to go back to him. I finally pulled myself together and went to his apartment.

The next morning I told Steve that I needed to go get my stuff from Tim's house. He reluctantly agreed to let me go after I called Tim's number and nobody answered. I went there that day and Tim's car was gone. When I let myself in the house, though, I discovered him sitting on the bed. All the charm was gone now; he was furious.

For the next two hours he angrily tried to convince me of what a mistake it would be to go back to Steve. He kept badgering me and I became confused. I knew full well what Steve was like and I didn't want to go back. Tim would vacillate between calm, reasonable arguments and tirades of anger. Finally, in a rage, he ripped my blouse off and forced himself on me. I was so weak and mousey at the time that I let him have his way. In some strange way, it was the thing that brought me back over to Tim.

At his insistence, I finally called Steve. "I don't love you anymore, I love Tim, and I'm not coming back," I coldly told him. When he heard that, he grabbed his off-duty revolver and spun the cylinder around in the mouthpiece so I could hear it. "All right, then you can listen to me blow my brains out!" he shouted.

"Steve, don't do it!" I yelled. When I said that, Tim grabbed my arm. I looked up at him to see the most evil look I had ever seen on anybody's face in all my life. "Kathy, if he wants to kill himself, let him do it. It's not your fault!" It was then I realized that this man I had taken for such a prince was full of the devil.

A pastor had arrived at Steve's apartment and got on the phone with me and asked if he could pray for me. I was terrified and just wanted to get out of that house, but was afraid to say anything. I told the pastor that I would meet him and Steve at his church and got off the phone. At first, Tim was adamant that I couldn't go, but he could see that I just wanted out of there and, finally, he relented. By the time I made it to where Steve was, it had been over six hours; six hours of hell for both of us.

It took this experience to see what Tim was really like, but it didn't make going back to Steve any easier. It was very difficult for a long time. For the first several months I felt like I had made a huge mistake and I was absolutely broken: broken over my sinfulness and the shame of being an adulteress, but also because my feelings for Steve were dead. I often felt I would rather be alone than to be with him. I could hardly take it when he would touch me.

To make matters worse, Steve was having a revival in his heart. He was on fire for the Lord and had now fallen deeply in love with me. The affection that I had wanted for so long was now mine in abundance. He was constantly wanting to hold my hand and hug me and kiss me—and I was sick. "Why couldn't you have been like this five years ago?" I would silently exclaim. There were many nights that I cried when we went to bed. I would make sure he didn't know because I didn't want to hurt him, but the truth was, I just didn't want him anymore. I constantly had to fight feelings of disgust.

Gradually, over the months, things got better. We both had so much to overcome. He still had some of the same old attitudes. There were times he would still blame-shift and manipulate, and sometimes even lash out in anger. In spite of his new-found passion for Jesus, he was also still struggling with pornography. But there was a brokenness in Steve now that had never been there before. God was winning in his life.

It took some time for my "feelings" to return. But, gradually they did. Actually, I think God destroyed the old foundation and built a new one, because, when the Lord restored the love and respect that I had lost for Steve, it came back in a brand new way. I started to respect and admire him more than I ever had before. There were times that my love for him became overwhelming; not in the idolatrous way it had been before, but in the love of the Lord. Over the years since we got back together, I have watched Steve allow God to humble him, correct him, and even crush him. Now he truly has become the man of my dreams.

But he wasn't the only one who needed to change. I had to learn to truly put God first in my life also. I came to realize that I had been just as consumed with Steve as he had been with sex. In my own self-centeredness, I had turned to one man after another, looking for fulfillment in life. I gradually learned to turn to God as the center of my life. This didn't make me love Steve less; it simply purified my love for him. Rather than a self-centered "love" which was given with the idea of having my own needs met, I learned to give my husband the unselfish love of the Lord. Our marriage grew stronger and stronger.

Almost immediately, Steve and I began spending time with the Lord every morning. This set a pattern that has lasted for many years. Being in touch with God everyday gave me a strength I had never known before. At first, as Steve continued struggling with his addiction to pornography, I became obsessed with his deliverance. God quietly began convicting me of this and kept leading me back to Himself. I soon discovered that the more connected I was with God, the more strength I had to help Steve with his problems.

As I continued to grow in the Lord, I was able to recognize the good that came of failure, instead of seeing it as a catastrophe. Because Steve was serious about his life with God, each fall back into sin served as a blessing in disguise. It deepened the hatred of his sin. Instead of falling apart when he would fail, I became an encouragement to him through those failures. The desire to be supportive of his efforts in this struggle and to keep him accountable in a loving way grew stronger. There was a time when I did not have the maturity or emotional strength to bear him in this way, but the closer I got to the Lord, the more I was able to handle. I came to realize that as long as Steve (or his victory) held the center-stage of my heart, my joy as a person would fall to pieces every time he would fail. But, as I increasingly allowed God the throne of my heart, I found that I now had the strength to help my husband through his failures.

A fling Steve took in May 1985, proved to be his last one. It took us some time to realize it, but he was free! Now things really began to change. He started becoming the strong one, spiritually. I could actually start leaning on him and confessing my faults to him. We reversed roles: he became my spiritual head and I became a wife who could submit to her "leader" with joy.

What a relief it was when I finally realized I no longer had to look over my shoulder. I still had to continue to repent of my own suspicious nature, but in my heart I knew we had crossed the deep waters of sexual addiction. Now we have a depth in our relationship that very few enjoy. Trusting God in going back to Steve was a turning point in my life, but it was also only the beginning of my own restoration. The restoration of our marriage came about because we both wanted God more than we wanted our own desires.

As I am rewriting this book (in 2003), it has now been eighteen years since that last fall on Steve's part, twenty-one since I reluctantly went back to him, and twenty-one since I married him. It was only a year after Steve's last fall in sin that God laid the burden on his heart to begin Pure Life Ministries. Since that time our love for God has intensified and our love for each other has deepened. What God has given me has been worth all of the grief I have endured through the years; not because of my happy marriage, but because of what I have in the Lord.

Writing this down in a book doesn't mean the story is over. I only see things getting better and better for both Steve and me, as we both continue to surrender ourselves to God, looking to Him to bring us the fulfillment we desire.

It certainly is true, that there is no pit so deep that the love of God isn't yet deeper.

HIS PRESENCE THROUGH PAIN

Dear Melody,

I don't mind it at all that you "dumped on me." I know
what it is like to have a "bad day" while facing such "waves
of pain" as you shared in your letter. You probably feel as
though you're drowning in an ocean of despair with no rescue
in sight. Believe me, I have been there many times in the past.
I wish I would've had someone to talk to when my waves hit.

I can understand your being baffled by all your troubles,
wondering "What is the point of it all?" At first glance, the
option to just throw up your hands and walk away seems
very appealing when you consider all the misery you're
likely to suffer by staying with your husband. But, let me
ask you something: what has kept you from giving up after
fifteen years of grief in this marriage? What has been your
motivation to hold on? I think you will agree with me that it's
more than simply your marital commitment and love for your
husband; there must be something deeper.

All these years you've been so focused on your husband's
unwillingness to change and have questioned why you even
continue to stay with him. Perhaps you've not given up
because deep in your heart you know that God is doing
something very wonderful inside of you. So despite how
much it hurts, you don't want to move from under the Potter's
hands.

Based on what you expressed in your letter, I know you
will understand what I'm about to share with you. The most
intimate and wonderful experiences that I have ever had with
the Lord happened when I was in the throes of total anguish
and absolute helplessness. What a bitter-sweet existence it
was during those times. Although I longed for the suffering
to end, I realized when it was over that I somehow lost that
abiding intimacy you're now experiencing with God. It is the

joy of such closeness that drives us to seek God through pain; there is nothing quite like it.

Often we hear nice sermons about God's love and faithfulness. Unfortunately, most of the time we try to understand His character with our natural reasoning minds. This, of course, hinders us from understanding God in our hearts. However, in the midst of your present circumstances, God is imparting to you a knowledge of Himself which simply cannot be learned through sermons or books. He is doing a deep and precise work in your soul, carefully molding you into the image of His Son, Jesus Christ. One day you will appreciate what God has done in your inward life— even more than you would ever appreciate having a "good marriage."

The apostle Paul, who endured many sufferings for Christ's sake, testified: "For just as the sufferings of Christ are ours in abundance, so also our comfort is abundant through Christ." (II Corinthians 1:5) We sense the presence of God in such a powerful way when He allows us to experience pain because our sights are fixed upon the One who is able to comfort us in all our distresses.

Another major blessing in all you're going through is the way the Lord will be able to use you one day to help others who are experiencing the same thing. In the same passage, Paul also said that our heavenly Father "comforts us in all our affliction so that we may be able to comfort those who are in any affliction with the comfort with which we ourselves are comforted by God." (II Corinthians 1:4)

This reminds me of the true story of Corrie and Betsy Ten Boom, two sisters who endured unspeakable suffering in a Nazi concentration camp during World War II. As Betsy was dying, she turned to Corrie and said, "We must tell them, Corrie—anyone who will listen. They will believe us because we have been there."

So, Melody, be encouraged and know that God is developing a powerful testimony in you. It is His sustaining power that is keeping you through the deepest waters. And you will discover that His love goes beyond any fleeting happiness resulting from favorable outward circumstances.

I pray that God will grant you the strength to hold onto that which now seems most painful but in the end will turn out to be that which best serves your soul.

THE HUSBAND'S STRUGGLE

Dear Miriam,

I can remember during the roughest years of my marriage feeling the same way as you do now. At times I was convinced that my husband was intentionally trying to drive me insane. Because I got stuck in my own little world, I lost a balanced perspective of others and life in general. Everything centered around how my husband's actions were affecting me. My pain and circumstances were big, while God was very small in my eyes. As a result, I rarely considered the needs of others— including my husband's desperate need for the Lord. I kept forgetting that his sin was destroying him also.

As difficult as it may seem, try and put yourself in his shoes for just a moment. Please understand that I wouldn't dare try to minimize or dismiss your husband's responsibility in this matter. Often, the last thing a man in sexual sin wants to do is own up to his own wrongdoings. However, for your sake, you should try to understand the assault he has come under in our sexually-oriented culture.

You mentioned once that Phil was exposed to pornography at a young age—this is one common denominator among sex addicts these days. Without a doubt, this exposure distorted his perspective of sexuality. And since then the choices he has made in life have led to his current bondage. But even so, it is easy to paint an unfaithful husband into an absolute monster without considering what has fueled his burning lust all these many years.

In our permissive society which says, "If it feels good, then do it!" women are presented as mere sex objects. Nowadays, little boys practically have no choice in the matter. They are constantly bombarded with "soft porn" everywhere—on TV, in magazines, at the mall, on billboards along the highway, in the check-out lines at grocery stores, and so on. Wherever they turn, they are assaulted with the message that pleasure is the purpose of life and that sex is the ultimate pleasure experience.

During his most impressionable years, the average boy is practically brainwashed by this message. As a result, he enters puberty full of curiosity and drawn to almost anything that has a sexual connotation. He is likely to begin masturbating as a relentless drive to have sex rages inside him. By this point, the young teen has stored up countless lustful images which help him to develop an elaborate fantasy life coupled with self-gratification. Then in high school, he learns how to get girlfriends, especially those most willing to give up their bodies.

By adulthood, he is practically a full-blown sex maniac. He discovers that his boyish curiosity has become a ravenous beast, always demanding more. No problem! The "red light" district offers him a wide selection of the hottest strip joints, massage parlors, and prostitution alleys if he can afford them. Do you know that pornography is a multi-billion dollar industry? It is more accessible than ever before because of the Internet—truly a "worldwide web" of evil. Men can now surf—or cruise, I should say—the net for pleasure without ever leaving home.

Many women lack compassion for their husbands' struggles because they have never been controlled by sexual desires themselves. The problem is that they don't understand how powerful the sexual drive is in a man and how susceptible he is to temptation in a culture that is full of sexual images.[*]

I hate to be so graphic, but it is important for you to see how easy the devil has made it for young men to become

---

[*] I highly encourage all wives to read my husband's book, *At the Altar of Sexual Idolatry* to gain tremendous insight into what the sexual addict experiences and what it will take for him to overcome the problem.

addicted to illicit sexual activity. In a sense, it shouldn't amaze any wife to discover that her husband struggles with sexual sin to some degree. In fact, it's a wonder that every man in America isn't a sex addict!

Being more aware of the enormous temptations that your husband must face every day will help you in a number of ways. First, you will realize that his addiction is definitely not your fault. Second of all, you will be more inclined to resist the self-righteous thinking that we women often give over to that "He just needs to exercise some self-control!" Thirdly, you will develop compassion in your heart toward him, which hopefully will calm any tempests of anger that would otherwise rule you. And finally, you will know exactly how to pray for him.

DEALING WITH SUSPICIONS

Dear Janet,

Your question concerning whether or not you should confront your husband because of your suspicions is a very good one. It is important that you first evaluate if your suspicions are based on actual facts or fear.

Men in sexual sin can be extremely smooth and very cunning. Most have perfected the art of deception and have led a double life for many years. Only the Lord knows the complete truth about what a man is doing in private. Therefore, the wife must really turn to Him for help in finding the truth about what's going on. I have experienced both sides of the coin: living in obsessive fear—just waiting for the next devastating revelation—and trustfully watching the Lord at work.

I can remember one experience in Los Angeles before Steve came to the Lord. He worked the night shift at the jail and usually got home by 8 a.m. But on one particular morning, I called him from my job several times. Each time, I got no answer. My heart started to sink. I knew something was wrong because he was in and out of sexual sin all the time back then. It was possible that he had gone to the store or somewhere else, but I sensed inside that he was up to no good. For me, his missing in action was a telltale sign that he was probably with a prostitute.

It wasn't until I got home that evening that I was able to talk to him. I didn't beat around the bush. I asked him straight out if he had been with someone else that day. Of course, he swore up and down that he hadn't, but I didn't believe him one bit. I continued to question him until finally he admitted that he had been with a prostitute that day.

In those days I couldn't discern the difference between when it was God revealing something to me and when it was just my own nagging suspicions. Often, when I had a gut feeling that he was being unfaithful, I was wrong.

Even after Steve came to the Lord and began to change, I was still overly suspicious. I was this way for years after he had been walking in victory. I conjured up all sorts of scenarios in my mind when he was alone or getting home late. Truthfully, I had become so paranoid and fearful during the years he was in sin that I believe the devil gained some kind of foothold in me. Had I verbalized all my inner fears, he and I probably would have ended up in divorce court once again.

My obsession with what he was doing, thinking, saying, plotting, and so on reinforced my fears. Whenever the phone rang, and I couldn't figure out whom he was talking to, I imagined it was a secret lover. Eventually, to my relief and embarrassment, it would end up being some friend of ours. My hyperactive imagination kept me in a prison of despair during this whole period.

How do you know if your misgivings are rooted in fear and influenced by the devil or if they are based upon fact and divinely inspired? Here's some questions you can ask yourself:

What has been your husband's track record during the last six months? Have you actually caught him in sin? Is there any evidence which definitely warrants your suspicions? For instance, has he been coming home late from work? Has money been disappearing that he can't account for? Does he give vague answers, or does he seem sincere? Has he been angry, defensive or combative like he may have been in the past? How does he treat you and the kids?

What about his walk with God? Does he seem hungry for the Lord? Does he look forward to going to church, or does he look for ways to get out of going? Does he spend time with the Lord each day? Is he reading his Bible? Does he spend hours sitting in front of the television?

We know a minister with the most lovable personality but

is the portrait of a deceiver. His wife never imagined the gross sin he was involved in (bestiality) by the way he treated her, the kids, and others. Fortunately, the Lord kept exposing his sin to her.

It is important for the wife to walk the fine line between trust and caution. One extreme keeps a wife in ignorance and the husband in his secret sin. The other extreme keeps the wife in a miserable life of fear which never disappears completely, no matter how hard the husband is trying.

I encourage you to use the questions listed above as tools to help you honestly evaluate your suspicions. If, after answering these questions, you still have nothing concrete to go on except a nagging sense that something is not right, get down on your knees before God. Deliberately put your husband in His hands. Then, ask Him to expose any secret sin that your husband might be involved in. Finally, pray that He sets you free from any life-dominating fear. Trust Him to answer your prayers.

WHY SHOULD I PUT UP WITH THIS?

Dear Lauren,

Y es, I agree that your life would probably be much easier without all of the heartache and grief of this marriage, but does having a comfortable, pain-free life mean so much to you that you would end your marriage for it? Does his pornography addiction really warrant divorce? I know you would agree that some things are important enough to fight for.

We will all face adversity and suffering in this world, simply because this world is, for the most part, in the hands of the enemy. How we respond to that pain will, to a large extent, determine the path our lives will take with God.

For the seeking heart, there is only one response: a humble willingness to submit one's grief-stricken heart into the hands of the Heavenly Father. This response comes from the desire to be more like Jesus. It is the submission of one's entire being into the life-changing processes of the Almighty.

Having a husband in sexual sin is both painful and humbling. It helps a woman see her own need for the Lord's help in her life. It is difficult to be in that place of helplessness and pain, and yet because God is drawn to the afflicted, His presence can make it a glorious place that nothing on earth can compare with. Make no mistake about it though, God uses this suffering to purify the woman of self-centeredness, self-righteousness and self-sufficiency. Through this fiery trial her compassion for the needs of others grows and matures. The wife who has been broken like this tends to see her husband's needs, rather than his failures.

There is another response to this suffering: a bitterness which is easy to justify when one has been hurt by the sin of another. It is easy for the wife to see herself as a victim of her husband's sin. This especially becomes true when she surrounds herself with others who treat her as a victim. Of course, it is true that in a very real way the wife is a victim of her husband's sin. However, it is important for the wife to remember that every human on the planet is a victim of the sin of others to one degree or another. It is an unavoidable part of life.

Bitterness causes a person to turn away from Jesus in the heart. Everything one does comes from the heart. How believers treat those who hurt them is an important aspect of Christianity. It should be remembered that our Savior was beaten, humiliated and murdered, and yet He never retaliated against His oppressors. Read the words of Peter regarding this subject:

> For this finds favor, if for the sake of conscience toward God a man bears up under sorrows when suffering unjustly. For what credit is there if, when you sin and are harshly treated, you endure it with patience? But if when you do what is right and suffer for it you patiently endure it, this finds favor with God.
>
> For you have been called for this purpose, since Christ also suffered for you, leaving you an example for you to follow in His steps, who committed no sin, nor was any deceit found in His mouth; and while being reviled, He did not revile in return; while suffering, He uttered no threats, but kept entrusting Himself to Him who judges righteously;
> (I Peter 2:19-23)

The Lord wants to comfort the wife in her suffering and then use that suffering to help her grow to be more Christ-like. But, if a woman never grows out of the place of seeing herself as a victim, nothing good will be accomplished in her life through it: she will have suffered for nothing! Instead of seeing the Lord with her through the whole ordeal, helping her, keeping her, sustaining her and molding her, all she can see is that she has been wronged by someone.

I believe that one reason God allows us to go through so much grief is so He can bring us into the light about what we are really like inside with the ultimate goal of making us more like Jesus. One illustration my husband Steve has used in the past is that of the tube of toothpaste. When you put pressure on it, the only thing that is going to come out of it is what's inside. Likewise, when affliction begins to squeeze us, what's inside is going to come out. Another illustration is that when the fire is put to the metal, the impurities rise to the top where they can be scooped off.

I believe that God is very intent on getting us to be real with Him and with ourselves. The days of superficial Christianity are coming to an end. He has to get us to look inside and see what we are really like so that we can repent and become the holy people He desires us to be.

I, too, suffered greatly at the hands of an unfaithful husband, but there came a time when I began to see beyond Steve's sin and started to recognize my own need for correction and help. Once I got a sight of that, my whole perspective changed. Now I can look back on this period of my life and can, with all sincerity, thank God for every bit of it. Why? Because this ordeal was the only way He was going to be able to help me in my own need. Before I went through this experience, my sense of need for God was very shallow, but the pain and rejection I experienced brought me to my knees and put something of depth in me that is worth everything I went through.

I realize that you have those around you who are encouraging the idea, "Why should I put up with this?" The answer to that question is twofold. First, you will endure the pain of your husband's mental infidelity because you want to extend the same mercy and forgiveness to him that the Lord has extended to you. Second, you would rather allow God to use this time to mold you into the image of Christ than to run from it. I hope this letter will encourage you to "bear all things, believe all things, hope all things, endure all things. Love never fails..." (I Corinthians 13:7-8)

THE ENCOURAGING WIFE

Dear Ann,

I appreciate so much your sincere desire to be a blessing
to your husband. Life's a lot easier when you have a husband
who is really trying to do what's right. The key to his living
victoriously is faithfulness and endurance. If he remains
diligent and chooses to do those things God has shown him,
he will make it!

Your role is to be his cheerleader, not just when he scores
a touchdown, but even after he fumbles the ball! Don't ever
hold his mistakes against him. As best as you can, create an
atmosphere of grace for him.* Let him know that you are
totally committed to him. No matter what kind of day he's
had, show him that you are in his corner. His sincere desire to
walk in victory will enable you to be completely supportive.

I'm glad to hear you are also being responsive to him
during intimate times. Many wives punish their husbands in
the bedroom by rejecting their advances.† However, what these
women don't realize is that this often make matters worse.
Generally speaking, the more satisfied a husband is at home, the
less inclined he is to search elsewhere! In I Corinthians 7:5 Paul
warns married couples: "Stop depriving one another, except by
agreement for a time that you may devote yourselves to prayer,
and come together again lest Satan tempt you because of your
lack of self-control."

Please continue to encourage your husband to have his
daily time with the Lord. As you know, it is essential that you
express support without nagging him. Perhaps you could even

---

* There is a fine line between allowing a husband to remain in sin and "creating an
atmosphere of grace." This husband's attitude allows for this (cf. letters to Judy and
Robin, pgs. 74 and 144).

† Again, there is another side to this. There are times when abstinence is the best
policy, especially when there is a legitimate fear of the husband transmitting an STD.

suggest that the two of you spend some time together in the Bible every evening.

As your husband matures in his walk with the Lord, one day he will cross a defining line—sexual sin will be completely behind him. I suspect that when that day comes he will gladly have this to say about his wife:

"Her children rise up and bless her; her husband also, he praises her, saying: 'Many daughters have done nobly, but you excel them all.' Charm is deceitful and beauty is vain, but a woman who fears the LORD, she shall be praised." (Proverbs 31:28-30)

THE ANGRY WIFE

Dear Deborah,

It is difficult to know how to respond to your letter. I am deeply grieved by the depth of your bitterness toward your husband. I got the impression that rather than looking for help, you simply wanted to unload all of the anger you feel toward him because of his unfaithfulness.

At any rate, I will try to filter through the bitterness you expressed in your letter, and I hope to say something that is both meaningful and helpful. My prayer is that you would allow God to soften your heart so that you can receive the breakthrough you desperately need. Your unwillingness to love your husband leaves no room for a God of love.

Jesus said, "For if you forgive men for their transgressions, your heavenly Father will also forgive you. But if you do not forgive men, then your Father will not forgive your transgressions." (Matthew 6:14-15)

This is where you have to begin: forgiveness. In order to be right with God yourself, you must be willing to forgive your husband regardless of the sins he's committed. Jesus says so!

Undoubtedly, you have been hurt in what is likely the most sensitive area of a woman's soul: your husband's devotion and faithfulness. The pain is real and the Lord understands the struggles a wife experiences with anger. When someone has been hurt like this, it is only natural to build walls around one's heart. However, Christians are still expected to obey God.

Many women have endured what you are suffering right now. It takes little effort to cave in to feelings of bitterness. It is so easy to hate when you've been hurt or violated in some way, but Jesus teaches us a better way to respond to such mistreatment: "Love your enemies..." (Matthew 5:44) To love the unlovable requires humility, longsuffering, and real strength of character.

Deborah, you can be free from your self-made prison today if you choose to repent of the hatred that has consumed your heart and then allow Christ to love your husband through you. Seems pretty impossible, huh? Not so! The reason you can do this is because Jesus showed us how. He was falsely accused, brutally beaten, and crucified between two criminals, but He never succumbed to the temptation to hate. Instead, He prayed for his persecutors while nailed to the cross. Therefore, because Jesus is our example, we can choose to be in that same Spirit rather than in the spirit of murder which is the hallmark of this world. There is nothing more God-like than forgiveness.

Pray this prayer now: Dear Lord, I repent of my bitterness, my hatred, my self-centeredness, and my pride. Please help me to learn from the example of Your suffering. Give me the desire and the power to forgive my husband. Help me to love him as You do. In Christ's Name, amen.

I FEEL LIKE I'M LOSING MY MIND!

Dear Anna,

*Y*ou have beautifully articulated the agony of countless women: "Is my husband a liar or am I just imagining all of this? I don't know what to believe anymore. I feel like I'm losing my mind!"

From what you expressed in your letter, it is obvious that your husband is manipulating you. You mentioned that every time you attempt to discuss his problems with him, he somehow twists the whole conversation around and makes you the focal point of the discussion, rather than him. You also said that when you confront him with undeniable evidence about his unfaithfulness, he manages to get everything so confused that you "don't know up from down."

Let me tell you: I've been there and done that! I experienced the same thing with Steve. Whenever I tried to talk to him about his involvement in sexual sin or even when he mistreated me, he would cleverly commandeer the conversation and somehow get the focus on me. To this day, I don't know exactly how he did it. Each time at the end of our discussion, I felt like I had made a big deal about nothing or that I was only imagining things.

One of the reasons he got away with this was because I desperately *wanted* to believe the best about my husband, which he was able to capitalize on with his strong, domineering personality. Using both his brute strength and his deceptiveness, he emotionally bullied me into submission with ease.

As it turned out, my suspicions were right on target. When I finally came to the realization that it was a hopeless cause to try to convince Steve to do the right thing, I simply left. I refused to accept his lies, his manipulation, and his sleeping around any longer. I knew that as long as I tolerated this from him he would remain unwilling to recognize his problem and deal with it.

Anna, you must be strong and take a firm stand in your dealings with Tony in the future. From what you shared in your letter, there is no question that he is being unfaithful to you. Since he isn't responding with sincerity to your discussions, you may consider getting a temporary separation from him. It could be just the jolt he needs! Ask the Lord to give you the wisdom to do what is right and the strength to follow through with whatever He lays on your heart to do.

JUST STOP IT!

Dear Janie,

I n your recent letter you asked, "Why can't he just stop it?" For us women who have never lived our lives just for sex, we cannot comprehend what is so difficult about saying "no" to sexual sin. It seems so simple—that it is only a matter of self-control. We often use such verses in the Bible that you quoted to strengthen our argument: "No temptation has overtaken you but such as is common to man; and God is faithful, who will not allow you to be tempted beyond what you are able, but with the temptation will provide the way of escape also, that you may be able to endure it. Therefore, my beloved, flee from idolatry." (I Corinthians 10:13-14)

You must understand that if it were easy for your husband to quit acting out, his problem would not be called an addiction. By definition addictive behavior is any uncontrolled habit which is difficult to give up, and it almost always leads to negative consequences. Take, for example, a young prostitute living on the streets of New York City who is addicted to crack cocaine. Perhaps at one point in time she anticipated a bright future ahead of her. However, over the years her life has become a vicious cycle of degradation and misery. To us, it seems so ridiculous for a woman to throw her life away like this because perhaps we don't understand the overwhelming power of sin. Or do we?

What about your bad habit of gossiping which you've repented of dozens of times? We often lack compassion for others who are bound up in some sin that we've never struggled with. It is quite easy to be self-righteous and point a condemning finger at someone with a life-dominating problem.

For years I was a compulsive spendthrift. I bought clothes, housewares, and anything that seemed like a bargain or a necessity. Without using much wisdom at all, I spent money frivolously and selfishly. But, because covetousness is rarely mentioned in the American Church, I was able to justify my overindulgences. Steve was bound in sexual sin, and I was hooked on wasting money on unnecessary things. In God's eyes I was a poor steward and just as unrighteous as he was—probably more so because of my self-righteousness.

The Scripture passage above applies to any true believer who has learned to appropriate the power of God in his life. However, anyone who comes to Christ after years of deep bondage must learn how to walk in the truth of these verses. The way of escape in the midst of overwhelming temptation is often unclear to an immature Christian.

Why doesn't your husband just stop? It sounds like he is sincerely trying to resist temptation. Change takes time. Failures can almost be expected along the way. Be patient and show him compassion. God is working in his life and it certainly seems as though he is responding. The day is quickly approaching when he *will* stop by the grace of God!

CONDEMNATION AND WORSHIP

Dear Karen,

I know just how you feel, questioning your walk with God because of the way you treat your husband at times. The Lord understands your struggle. So don't be overly hard on yourself.

Each of us was born with a sinful nature. However, whenever we hurt or offend others, we can repent to them and to God and try our best not to do so again. This is all the Lord expects from us. In return, our sins are not only covered, but they are placed in the sea of forgetfulness.

Your question, "How can I worship the Lord when I'm so evil inside?" shows that you don't have a full understanding of your relationship with God. As Christians we often fall prey to the misconception that we must first be completely obedient before we dare come into His presence. There is some degree of truth to this. We must never come before the Almighty's throne room in a presumptuous or irreverent manner.

Please keep in mind that our heavenly Father knows that we are human and that we often miss the mark. Nevertheless, He loves us and longs to have unbroken fellowship with us. When we worship Him from our hearts, we are united with Him spiritually, much like when a married couple makes love to one another.

Unfortunately, many people put the cart before the horse so to speak. They think that they must become holy before they can be intimate with God. Not so! When we come humbly before the Lord, by His grace we are allowed entrance into His holiness, which makes us *want* to do what is right.

However, the devil tries to convince us that we must first punish ourselves before God will even hear our prayers. When we believe this blatant lie, we are our own judges. Our relationship with the Lord becomes completely based upon our performance level (i.e., works). We are then the center rather than Jesus—this is precisely the devil's goal. But the truth of the matter is that when we confess our sins, He is faithful and just to forgive us and will cleanse us from all unrighteousness. (I John 1:9)

We teach the men in the live-in program to come into the meetings ready to worship God—even if they acted like the devil himself fifteen minutes before the meeting! The best way to break free of a devilish spirit is to repent and enter into the Spirit of the Lord. Repentance not only involves us turning away from sin but it also means that we turn toward God.

You struggle over the bitterness you feel when your husband is unfaithful to you in his heart. The best remedy to bitter water in the well is to flush it out with the Water of Life! Karen, some of my most liberating experiences occurred when I found a quiet place to shut out all of the distractions of the world, got on my knees, and began to tell Jesus how much I loved Him.

Although most of my two hours with the Lord in the morning is spent in prayer and Bible study, I also try to spend time just worshipping Him. I particularly enjoy the music of Hillsong and Vineyard, because these groups seem to have a real anointing at leading others into a heart-felt adoration of God.

There have been times I have become so overwhelmed with God's goodness that I've ended up with my face buried in the carpet weeping. On other occasions I became so exhilarated with Him that I had to dance! I love to worship Jesus and tell Him how much I love Him and appreciate all that He's done for me.

Several wives have commented that they would express such gratitude only if their marriages were restored. But let me tell you: it's simply not true. If you don't learn how to worship God and thank Him in the midst of trials, you will never do so with sincerity once they're over. The more you worship God, the more you will want to worship Him regardless of your circumstances. So when you feel like there's nowhere else to turn, you can find shelter and have fullness of joy in the presence of the Lord.

Please remember that the Lord longs to be with you, in spite of your failures. Just repent and enter in!

THE WRONG OBSESSION

Dear Bernice,

I understand your deep desire to see your husband repent so that your fractured marriage might be healed. However, I suspect that you are making the same mistake I once made: obsessed with seeing it happen.

Solomon said, "Hope deferred makes the heart sick." (Proverbs 13:12) Just as your husband's preoccupation with sex will leave him empty and miserable, your obsession will do the same for you.

It is much better (and wiser) to focus your attention on the Majestic One, the Alpha and Omega, the Ancient of Days. He alone can fill the void in your heart and comfort you in the midst of your sorrow. He alone can soothe and suture your jagged wounds. His joy is your strength! (Nehemiah 8:10)

You must keep in mind that God is training you. You want everything to be made right, but the Lord is not thinking along those lines. It is more important to Him that you have something of substance inside you that is of Him. His concern is for your eternal well-being, not necessarily your temporal happiness. You have become frantic in your efforts to store up treasures on earth, but Bernice, those treasures are susceptible to moth and rust. God is trying to give you eternal riches.

I, too, saw my husband's sin as an unwelcome interruption in the "happily-ever-after" life I had dreamed we would have together. But how grateful I am today for all the good that came out of it! I am so thankful that God didn't just wave a magic wand and give me what I wanted, what I pleaded for at times. Each step of the way He lead me into something I desperately needed: true intimacy with Him. So I encourage you to keep your eyes focused upon the Lord and allow Him to do the wonderful work inside you that you really need.

TOO MANY VOICES

Dear Cynthia,

I t is difficult to imagine how hard it must be to have a family so against your marriage. When you married James, you entered into an exclusive relationship that no one else has any right to. You will have to be the one who establishes this fact with your family members, who apparently feel it is their place to dictate to you how you should handle your marriage.

In Genesis, the Lord said, "For this cause a man shall leave his father and mother, and shall cleave to his wife: they shall become one flesh." (Genesis 2:24) The same holds true for the daughter who marries.

It can be so confusing when we listen to too many voices. Everybody has an opinion about how you should handle a particular situation—usually, everyone's opinion is different. It is rare to meet a family which can be objective and supportive when they see a loved one hurt or in trouble.

Why does your family want you to divorce James? How will that help you? Is that what God is saying to you? Sometimes well-intentioned family members do not realize the true condition of their own hearts—that they are self-righteous and are subject to sin themselves.

I strongly urge you not to allow your father and mother to advise you, since they have shown themselves to be angry and bitter against a brother in the Lord.

If your stand for your marriage causes your relationship with your family to break down, you may be forced to decide which is more important to you. One thing I can assure you is, if there is even the slightest hope left for your marriage, then God is for it. Stick to His counsel and listen to His voice.

I hope this will prove to be an encouragement to you.

FILLING THE VOID

Dear Susan,

I really appreciate how you poured your heart out in your letter. I know firsthand what it's like to pursue worthless things in order to bring momentary fulfillment.

During the early years of my marriage, I wasted countless hours and spent hundreds of dollars just to make myself feel better. Why? Well, most of the time I felt empty and alone. My life seemed meaningless. So, out of desperation I tried to fill the void through shopping. I was never satisfied with what I had. A part of almost every paycheck was spent on some new outfit. I had to have my hair and nails done frequently. Later, I was into interior decorating. I was on a mission to spruce up our home. I constantly bought new furniture and little knickknacks here and there. Whenever I purchased something new, whether it was an outfit or a living room set, I felt wonderful for a couple of days. Then, the feelings of emptiness would return and remain until the next shopping spree. Now, in retrospect, I see that the more I bought, the emptier I felt inside.

At the time, it never even occurred to me that I might be doing something that displeased God. Of course, buying a new skirt is not a sin. However, in reality I had become just as obsessed with spending money as my husband was with sex. While my sin seemed innocent compared to his, both were idolatrous attempts to fill a void which only Jesus could satisfy.

As I matured and came into a deeper understanding of God, He mercifully began to convict me of my excessive spending. I saw how I had turned to worldly pleasures in my pain rather than to Him. I had minimized and even justified my splurging because of all the agony my husband put me through. Nevertheless, just as it took years for him to overcome the tremendous stronghold of sexual lust, it took some time for me to break free of my own covetousness.

Since then, having a relationship with the Lord has brought great meaning to my life. I love my husband and never want to revisit those painful years I left behind, but the joy that fills my heart comes from what I have in God—not in the things this world has to offer. I hope and pray that you also will discover the true Source/Wellspring of all fulfillment: just Jesus, Himself.

THE TV BATTLE

Dear Patricia,

*I*n your letter to me you expressed: "It makes me mad that I can't watch television because of my husband's sin. It's just not fair! I feel that, if he's got a problem with it, he should just leave the room."

You also mentioned that your husband felt convicted about watching TV after he read about its effects on the Christian in *At the Altar of Sexual Idolatry.* I won't take the time here to mention all its ungodly influences which my husband expressed in his book, but I will say that it negatively affects all believers—not just those struggling with sexual sin. Basically, TV does far more to draw believers away from God than toward Him. How much more so for the man struggling with lust!

I realize that you have had to withstand the brunt of your husband's reckless folly and that it seems like you're being punished for his sin. I know it's been difficult for you, but can you see that he is now sincerely trying to do the right thing? I think your husband's attempts to consecrate himself to the Lord are highly commendable. There are many women out there who wish their husbands were more willing to face their problems and let God deal with them.

I know you weren't expecting a response like this, but I want to encourage you to lay aside your own desires and go to the Lord with an open heart. God is always fair and knows what's best for you. Not only will He lead you in the right way, but He will make it a pleasure for you when you obey Him.

FRUITS OF REPENTANCE

Dear Pam,

I would like to respond to your question, "How can I know that my husband has truly repented?" Repentance is, of course, absolutely essential to overcoming sin.

Unfortunately, many of those in sexual sin never experience true repentance. Although they may cry over their sin, plead with God to set them free, and make determined "efforts" at achieving victory or solemn vows to never go back, they haven't truly had an inward change of heart.

I remember a couple named Bill and Fran we counseled some time ago. They had been married eight years and had two small children by the time Bill entered our live-in program. He had a track record of unfaithfulness. Like so many men in sexual sin he would seemingly do good for some time but would then go on another binge of sexual sin. Each time the tears of sorrow and promises of "I'll never do it again!" would stream forth. "I don't know why God won't set me free!" Bill would protest. "I'm doing everything I know to do to get victory," he would exclaim with a tinge of resentment toward the Lord. Fran even found herself getting angry with God because she was so convinced that her husband had sincerely repented.

During this whole period Bill had led Fran to believe that his problems were limited to pornography. However, he had been unfaithful to her, visiting prostitutes. It was only by chance -- divine chance, that is—that she found out about Pure Life Ministries at the same time she discovered all of this.

Immediately, Fran gave him an ultimatum. "That's it, Bill! You either go to Pure Life or we're through!" she angrily told him. Bill complied with her wishes to come into the live-in program and assured the staff that he sincerely wanted help.

Generally, when a new guy comes into our program, the Pure Life counselors can quickly figure out what his problems are, how well he will get along with the others in the program, and how cooperative he will be with the staff. What takes time to really discern is how serious he is about overcoming sin, way down in his heart. Eventually, if he remains in the program long enough the truth comes out.

It took quite some time to figure Bill out. He was a real challenge because he was so good at presenting a false image—he even had our counselors fooled for awhile. But our staff understands how deceptive these men can be because they themselves have lived in the same deception before coming on staff. They know that there are some men they just cannot figure out without the help of the Holy Spirit.

For several weeks, Bill did everything right in the live-in program. He did his homework—earnestly. He did what his counselors told him to do. He listened attentively to the messages preached in our chapel services. He continually expressed a desire to mature as a Christian, but still, he had not experienced any real breakthroughs. Was there a lack of motivation? Was he still clinging to some secret sin? Did he have a hidden agenda? Only time would tell.

Before long, we began suspecting that Bill's tearful bouts of repentance were insincere. Then one day we found out that he had been coming on to some woman at his job. It became clear to us all that, despite all of his protests to the contrary, he simply wasn't truly repenting of his sin. He had been willing to obey God only to a certain extent but balked when God started asking for a full surrender.

A man's sincerity level is much more difficult to ascertain when he is at home. It takes some men time to come out of the clutches of sexual sin. But I am convinced, that there isn't a sincere man alive, who couldn't overcome his sin at the Pure

Life live-in program. I say this because everything he needs to find victory is made available to him: a godly environment, counselors who have been there and who offer wisdom to overcome life-dominating sin, tight accountability, and most of all, a heightened sense of the presence of God.

Bill's insincerity became obvious after Fran served him his divorce papers and he quit the live-in program. There was no longer a reason to continue the charade.

Repentance often comes in stages. A man who has been deeply entrenched in sexual sin will have years of ingrained habits to contend with. He will struggle with feelings of hopelessness, which paralyze even the most well-intentioned. All of this is in addition to the great love he has had with his sin. But, nevertheless, if he is sincere, changes will begin to occur as he is given new direction and real hope through Jesus Christ.

We encourage wives to look for *fruits* of repentance, as John the Baptist called them. There should be some evidence that genuine effort is being put forth. Once your husband sets himself on the right course to victory—walking in daily repentance, spending time in the Word and in prayer, staying accountable, and loving others (especially his wife)—God will take him across a line. The day will come when God will get him to a place spiritually where he can make that final surrender and consecration, and he will do it.

The fruits of repentance are positive indicators that a real heart transformation is underway. Watch for them, and you will get a better idea of your husband's level of commitment.

CONFRONTING THE HUSBAND

Dear Joyce,

Perhaps it's time to confront your husband. His continuing to view pornography and then lying about it warrants your taking some serious action.

In Matthew 18, Jesus lays out the framework for proper biblical confrontation. He said, "And if your brother sins, go and reprove him in private; if he listens to you, you have won your brother. But if he does not listen to you, take one or two more with you, so that by the mouth of two or three witnesses every fact may be confirmed. And if he refuses to listen to them, tell it to the church; and if he refuses to listen even to the church, let him be to you as a Gentile and a tax-gatherer." (Matthew 18:15-17)

You shared in your letter that you had tried, on three separate occasions, to talk with Pete about his problem. Each time he was very defensive and argumentative. In the words of Jesus, he didn't "listen to you."

So now your next step is to approach him with one or two other believers. For starters, I suggest that you make an appointment with your pastor. Explain to him your situation and ask him to speak with your husband. I only say this because your husband attends church and considers himself a Christian.

If your pastor is unwilling to get involved, don't give up! Search for a godly person you both respect, perhaps a close friend or an elder of the church.

More than likely your husband will become angry and see this as an invasion of privacy. No doubt such exposure will be humiliating to him. At any rate, it is important for you to be strong and compassionate through the whole ordeal. As you prepare to do this, you will face a strong temptation to call the whole thing off. Resist it! You will do him a tremendous disservice if you continue to ignore his hypocrisy. If his wife won't love him enough to confront him, who will?

Don't feel guilty for bringing others into this. It would be unmerciful on your part if you cover up for him and pretend that everything is fine. Again, he may get upset with you, but that's all right. I don't mean to be insensitive, but he will get over it. Joyce, you must keep a proper perspective: your husband's soul could be at stake here. A severe blow to his pride is one of his greatest needs, and his hurt feelings are only a minor consequence in the whole scheme of things. You see, you cannot allow him to use anger or resentment to dominate the situation. For his sake, you must remain rational and be firm with him no matter how he responds. This way you have a better chance at salvaging your marriage. Let's pray that your husband will WAKE UP out of the delusion that he can participate in such darkness and still think that he's walking with the Lord.

As far as a separation is concerned, I advise you to give this a little time and see how he responds after you confront him. It would not be wise to threaten him with a separation, unless you are prepared to follow through and accept all the ramifications this would entail. However, if nothing has changed after a month or so, you should consider taking stronger measures.

I will be praying for you and hope that the Lord will open Pete's eyes.

THE ABUSIVE HUSBAND

Dear Elaine,

*I*t sounds as though you and your kids are in an extremely volatile situation. Not only is your husband addicted to pornography, insanely jealous, and very controlling, but he is physically and emotionally abusive.

The key word here is CONTROL. Your husband is using his temper to manipulate and control you. You are emotionally beaten down and thoroughly intimidated by him.

Elaine, many women stay in unhealthy relationships, like yours. In some "sick" way, they start to feel as though they need the approval of the abuser. The more disapproval these women receive through anger and perhaps even through violence, the more pronounced their desire becomes to win back the approval that they've lost. Somehow they become addicted to the entire abusive process which involves a hopeless merry-go-round of manipulation and selfishness on the part of their abusers and theirs as well. It sounds like this describes your situation. Please allow me to give some helpful advice:

You must first take control of the situation. *You* are allowing your husband to control you with his anger. This keeps you beaten down and unable to find God for yourself. It also keeps him from seeing his desperate need for God.

I believe your circumstances are severe enough to warrant an immediate separation from him as well as a restraining order. If you are fearful of him because of his violent, controlling nature, I suggest that you take the kids and leave when he's at work. (You might check with an attorney before pursuing this course of action.)

Once you've left, be aware of the fact that you will naturally start to crave his affection and attention again. You will probably second-guess your decision to leave. An overwhelming sense of insecurity may rise up within you.

This may prompt you to remember his positive side or even reminisce about your happiest moments with him. Meanwhile, your memory of his abusiveness will fade. If you feel an overwhelming temptation to contact him "just to see how he's doing," resist it! Don't be caught off guard! The less contact the better.

You should also be aware of the fact that you will probably feel a sense of guilt over leaving him. It is important that you remember that he has caused this separation; not you. Again, resist such feelings.

Give him a few days to simmer down and allow reality to settle in. When you speak to him, be calm and aloof. Don't talk to him if he is in a rage, and don't let him sweet-talk you into coming home right away. Remember: he's a controller and will use every angle possible in order to get his own way. Just cut him off and keep the conversation strictly business (i.e. controlled visits with the kids, bills, and etc.). Once you have left, you will have control of the situation. Don't give it up!

In time, if he truly repents and turns to the Lord, his frantic efforts to get you back will be replaced with a new passion for Jesus. This is what you're looking for: "fruits of repentance."

I'm not suggesting divorce, but I do feel that it isn't safe for you or the kids to stay with your husband the way he is now. The key is to stay turned to the Lord through the entire process. Only He can give you the strength you need to break free of this unhealthy relationship. And also, with you out of the way, God will have a better chance at reaching your husband's heart.

It may take time for him to change. At any rate, you must make a real commitment to trust the Lord to work things out, no matter how long it takes. Be encouraged and know that God is ultimately the One in control and that nothing is too difficult for Him. It is my testimony that God can take the worst thing and make it better than if it had never happened.

WHERE IS GOD?

Dear Jenny,

It's been five years since I've heard from you. You were then seven years into your marriage. I am sorry to hear that he has plunged deeper into his sin and remains unrepentant. This still baffles you and makes you wonder "Where is God?" in all of this.

So for twelve years now, it seems that your prayers have been in vain—that God has turned a deaf ear. Jenny, this is not true! He is attentive to your cries and is always there going through it with you. He knows more than any of us what it's like to be mistreated by the one He loves. For centuries God has had to patiently suffer the rejection and unfaithfulness of His children. Nevertheless, His heart is just the same now as it always has been: "O My people, how I yearn for you and long for you to return to Me." His motives are by no means selfish but for their good. Still, they continue to break His heart as they pursue pleasure and fulfillment apart from Him. This keeps them in chains. He wants to set them free, but they prefer bondage instead. Does this sound at all familiar?

Your situation may fit within the framework of "biblically permissible divorce," but I will never advise you to divorce him. Only God knows your husband's heart. Who's to say that he might repent next week? The Lord alone can lead you in this matter.

Perhaps it would be a good idea for you to go away for a few days to seek the Lord. This way you won't be immersed in all the oppression and circumstances which stem from your husband's infidelity. Your mind will become much clearer, and your time with God will prove to be fruitful. Hopefully, you'll be able to get a clear leading from Him about what to do.

Many people would consider you a fool for staying with Joe. I, for one, admire your courage and determination to stand in the gap for him and for your marriage. Based upon our previous conversations, I don't believe that you are taking a stand out of some selfish "neediness" but simply because temporal happiness is not the number one priority in your life.

Your patience and longsuffering with Joe is a picture of how Jesus lays down His life for us everyday. What a different sense I got from a Christian radio program I heard one day. A hurting wife was in a similar predicament as yours, and the radio host blasted over the air: "Get on with your life, because God wants to use you." This was very disturbing to me. What about "until death do us part?" What about exploring the possibility of reconciliation? What about compassion and forgiveness? What about the love of Christ? These days it seems that our comprehension of true Christianity is becoming more and more shallow as the love of many grows colder. (Matthew 24:12) Much of so-called Christian counseling is actually based upon worldly ideas and principles which emphasize protecting oneself at any expense. Psychology tends to emphasize personal happiness over true obedience to Christian principles.

Nevertheless, Jenny, you keep trusting the Lord to lead you. His promises are sure and true, and His counsel stands forever. Continue to seek His face with all your heart and know that He has promised never to desert you nor forsake you.

VAGUE SUSPICIONS

Dear Laura,

$\mathcal{Y}$ou shouldn't be surprised to be feeling nagging suspicions. You have been through a lot with your husband. Over a long period of time he had several affairs, been involved in all types of perversion, and kept it completely hidden until you caught him. Your lack of trust for him is understandable, but I think I can share some things that will help you.

First, because you've been deeply hurt by his behavior, you will naturally tend to imagine the worse-case scenario. If you allow your mind to run wild, you will imagine him to be in bed with some woman every time he's away from home. Realize that just because such thoughts come into your mind doesn't mean that they're legitimate.

Second, you mentioned that your husband has kept a good track record ever since he repented. There is no indication that he's been unfaithful to you in quite awhile. He's been honest about his failures. He continues to press into God. You no longer see him leering at women when you're together. Although he still has his struggles from time to time, it sounds like he's doing great overall.

Third, you must remember that there is an active agent involved in your situation who wishes to sabotage your marriage: the devil. He is known as "the accuser of the brethren" and delights in planting accusatory thoughts in a wife's mind about her husband. Look for him to bring to your mind memories of past painful experiences in an attempt to torment you and to stir up suspicion.

Therefore, it's very important that you constantly guard your thought life. I know how easy it is to sit and imagine the worst—it comes natural with little effort at all. But living inside you is the Holy Spirit of God who enables you to believe the best. This requires much discipline on your part.

Out of obedience to the Lord you must examine and bring every thought into captivity. (II Corinthians 10:5) Are they true? Are they honorable? Are they right? Are they pure? Are they lovely? Are they of good repute? (Philippians 4:8)

We wives need to know that when we allow fear and doubt to consume our minds we become just as self-centered as the man who is controlled by lust. Why? Because when we do, we are only thinking about ourselves, and everything centers around us. So, the next time those dark, sneaking suspicions start to invade your mind, immediately get out of yourself by interceding for your husband. In other words, pray instead of think! If you will practice this, gradually you will become victorious in the way you think and will be more inclined to trust your husband. Furthermore, your prayers will help your husband attain real victory. The loser will be the devil who will grow discouraged and flee from you since his accusations will serve only to stimulate your prayer life!

FEAR OF OTHER WOMEN

Dear Rachel,

I appreciate your letter of apology. I know you are trying to grow in the Lord but still make mistakes like all of us. Perhaps we can use this situation as a springboard to help you with some of your struggles.

Of course, the comment you made in your first letter that I must "love being surrounded by all these men" at the live-in facility was quite upsetting to me. To tell the truth, living here for several years, ministering to men who come from sordid backgrounds and whose hearts are full of every kind of perversion imaginable, has been extremely difficult. Please understand that I love my husband and have no interest in gaining the attention of your husband or any other man for that matter. But this letter is about you, not me.

I believe that your fear of other women precipitated your comment. Fear can cause people to say and do very cruel and unpleasant things because it is inherently *self*-protective. The greater the fear in a woman's heart, the greater the potential she has of hurting others in *self*-defense.

It is fairly apparent that you are intimidated and even feel threatened by other women. This is partly due to the pain you've suffered because of Ed's struggles with lust. Nevertheless, your problems are not based in Ed's heart but your own.

I have good news for you: there is a way out of the self-imposed prison of fear that has kept you bound! The apostle John said that it is love which casts out fear. (I John 4:18) As you allow the Lord to love others through you, gradually your fear of other women will fade away.

Let me give you some practical steps to help you break free of this bondage. First, you must acknowledge that your "spirit of fear" is sinful and *repent* of it. Humble yourself before the Lord and confess to Him how *self*-absorbed you are. Repent of this selfish attitude and a lack of concern for the welfare of others. Then ask Him to help you to change.

Second, when you're around another Christian woman and you begin to sense fear welling up inside, make an effort to go to her and strike up a friendly conversation. This will help to weaken and perhaps even dispel the paralyzing fear you struggle with. I realize the feelings can seem overwhelming at times, but at some point you will need to get beyond feelings and begin to enter into a life of faith in God. He will help you as you turn to Him.

Third, you must realize that having suspicious thoughts is part of your sinful nature and that the devil loves to torment you whenever you give in to these thoughts. For this reason, you must begin to exercise mental self-control. How do you do this in a practical way? Focus your attention and energy on meeting the needs of others around you. Pray for others throughout the day—especially your husband! Get involved in an auxiliary at your local church. Be a volunteer at a local nursing home.

Rachel, I urge you to do the things I have suggested to you and turn to the Lord. He wants to set you free! Remember: God has not given you a spirit of fear "but of love and power and a sound mind." (II Timothy 1:7)

ABANDONED BY GOD

Dear Shirley,

I received your letter about a week ago and have been praying about how to respond to it.

I can relate to your feeling that God has abandoned you. I don't endorse it by any means but I do understand it because I went through the same thing.

Let me briefly share with you my own testimony. My number one question for many years was: Why did God let me marry this guy when He knew what he was like?

I was not a Christian when Steve and I met, but after several months of living with him, I came to the Lord and gave Him my whole heart. I left Steve the next day. I was on fire for God. I loved the Lord and had no interest in a relationship. For the first time in my life, I was happy and fulfilled as a single Christian. Then one day, after many months of walking with Jesus, I felt led to call Steve up to share the Lord with him.

At the end of a very awkward and difficult conversation, a man who was cold, hard-hearted, and angry toward God told me that I should pray about marrying him. Can you imagine: a proposal from a God-hater? I was in shock, yet somehow I sensed that was exactly what the Lord wanted me to do. I can't explain it.*

Even while I was dating Steve, I had no idea that he was being unfaithful to me. But God knew beforehand all of the horrible grief I would eventually suffer in my marriage with Steve—the pain and disgrace I would endure. Why didn't He prevent all this?

---

* The Bible is very clear that believers should not be yoked with unbelievers (II Corinthians 6:14) and I have heard countless heartbreaking stories of women who went against this biblical command. However, when dealing with spiritual matters, sometimes God's dealings with His children cannot be neatly fit in a tidy package. I know I was created to be Steve Gallagher's wife.

It would have been very easy for me to be mad at God, considering the fact that this was my second marriage that seemed destined for divorce court. I was oblivious to the future plans and purposes of God concerning Steve and me. All I could foresee was a trail of tears and endless suffering. There were times God appeared to be far, far away. However, He was there throughout the whole ordeal, suffering with me.

There is a similar story of infidelity in the Bible. I'm referring to Hosea and Gomer. Hosea was also told by God to marry someone who would prove to be unfaithful: "Go, take to yourself a wife of harlotry." (Hosea 1:2) He obeyed the LORD and had to bear her unfaithfulness for years, but God had a bigger plan in mind.

What if I wouldn't have married Steve? Yes, such a choice possibly could have saved me a lot of grief with him, but who's to say I would have ended up in a situation any less painful? Not only that, I would have missed the eternal work God desired to do in me through the experience. No matter whom I might have eventually married, I never could have ended up with a more wonderful marriage than the one I now have with Steve.

Whatever happens in your situation, Shirley, know that your heavenly Father is right there with you. He will *never* abandon you and will always give you the grace to endure any suffering He allows in your life. Just purpose in your heart to seek His face like never before. Not only will you find comfort and strength in your times of weakness, but you will discover that God's grace is truly sufficient for you.

BEARING THE BURDEN

Dear Clara,

$\mathcal{I}$ can certainly empathize with your feeling as if you're weighed down under a thousand pounds. Having a husband who is addicted to sex can be an enormous burden.

As a wife and mother, you feel obligated to be the spiritual leader of the home, since your husband is incapable of assuming that role. Consequently, the welfare of the entire family rests upon your shoulders. Some husbands are rendered so helpless by their sin that they require the care and attention one naturally gives to a child. Who will do this for him if not the wife? She must shoulder all of these responsibilities as well as deal with her own pain, fear, and emotional needs.

Some women with strong dispositions are not easily shaken and do remarkably well under constant pressure. Others, however, become overwhelmed and usually collapse under the weight of it sooner or later. Whatever the case may be, it is vital that a hurting wife learn how to take everything to the Lord in prayer. Even the most resilient will at some point handle their husbands wrongly, if they rely on their own strength.

The psalmist said, "Cast your burden upon the LORD, and He will sustain you; He will never allow the righteous to be shaken." (Psalm 55:22) He also said, "Blessed be the Lord, who daily bears our burden, the God who is our salvation." (Psalm 68:19)

The key to allowing the Lord to be your Burden Bearer is to stay in constant fellowship with Him. If you learn to abide in the presence of Jesus, He will grant you the grace which will make your burdens become lighter.

Do you remember the story of Mary and Martha found in Luke 10? There was Martha in a frenzy, anxiously running about trying to keep things together while her sister sat at the Master's feet. Jesus said to her, "Martha, Martha, you are worried and bothered about so many things; but only a few things are necessary, really only one, for Mary has chosen the good part, which shall not be taken away from her."

Sometimes it seems so difficult to sit at His feet when you feel overwhelmed by problems. The alternative though, is to carry that weight by yourself. If you do, you will most likely end up frustrated and angry.

Don't get me wrong: it is right that a wife bears her husband's burdens rather than ignore or disregard them. However, she must carry them only as far as the throne of the Almighty. It is a wife's duty to battle through spiritually for her husband which can only be done on her knees before the Lord.

To sum it up, Clara, make it a daily practice to cast "all your care upon him; for he careth for you." (I Peter 5:6-7) Pray earnestly for your husband, and then leave the worries at God's throne. As you learn to do this, you will become like Mary, finding the joy of the Lord's presence in the midst of your storm.

THE ROOTS OF HOMOSEXUALITY

Dear Janice,

I'm so sorry to hear about your husband's decision to "come out of the closet." How tragic it is that he chose to give over to the feelings he has suppressed for years rather than seek help. I will attempt to answer your question regarding where these "feelings" originated.

There are a number of factors that may contribute to a man being sexually attracted to other men.

Many seem to be "born that way." Researchers claim that they can prove that some men have a certain genetic predisposition toward homosexuality. We have had many homosexuals tell our counselors that they had felt this same-sex attraction for as long they could remember. Undoubtedly man's genetic pool has been corrupted by the fall in the Garden in ways that we don't understand. Every person has inherent lust for sin he must conquer in life. Our fallen natures make us all predisposed toward certain types of sin. The fact that there would be those predisposed toward homosexual sin shouldn't surprise us.

Many others who become homosexuals, come from the stereotypical family where there is a strong mother and a weak or absent father. This setting seems to create a need inside a little boy in his formative years, which can later compel him to seek acceptance through sexual activity with men.

Others develop homosexual lust as a result of being molested as young boys or through experimentation in adolescence or teenage years. The lust, introduced early on, is cultivated as he grows older. Another group that fits into this category are heterosexual men who regularly view pornographic materials, especially videos. As they watch men and women have sex, a lust for other men begins to grow in their hearts.

Regardless of how a man acquires homosexual lust, he

still has a *choice* as to whether he will give himself over to it or not. As I have stated earlier, every one of us is predisposed toward some sin. James said, "But each one is tempted when he is carried away and enticed by his own lust." (James 1:14) There are a myriad of sins and countless different lusts to provoke them. Sexual lust is only one of many. Consequently, the *origin* of the homosexual sin isn't important. We all have a free will and must choose to obey or disobey God's Word.

I understand your struggles with the unfairness of it all. "My husband didn't ask to have these feelings. It just doesn't seem fair!" Janice, is it fair that a little girl is born blind? Is it fair that a little boy is born addicted to crack? Is it fair that another is mentally retarded? I could go on and on, of course. The human race has been messed up ever since the fall of our first parents in the Garden. Furthermore, we have to remember that since then this world has been controlled by a very evil presence—the devil and his angels. He is called a murderer and destroyer for good reason.

But glory to God! We have a faithful, loving Father who is ever ready to lead us into the abundant Christian life if we will only turn to Him with all of our hearts. There is no reason for anybody to live out his life on this earth in misery, no matter how bad his circumstances or struggles are.

You must realize that your husband has never truly yielded his heart to God. He has gone through the motions of Christianity, but hasn't given his all to the Lord. Therefore, he has been unable to appropriate all that God had for his life. His lack of real commitment has resulted in a lack of real victory. Finally, in self-pity, he has thrown in the towel to pursue and fulfill his lustful desires, having convinced himself that he had given God every opportunity to set him free.

Pray that he will soon come to see the emptiness of the homosexual lifestyle and then will repent and seek God with all of his heart.

THE APPEASING WIFE

Dear Judy,

What a tragic story you shared with me: years of emotional and physical abuse by a controlling and domineering husband, only to end in divorce because of his unwillingness to repent. For what it's worth, I just want to tell you that I think you did the right thing. Your husband was sexually involved with other women, he was abusing you and your children, and he showed no inclination whatsoever that he was willing to change.

In your letter, you expressed how terribly you regret that you didn't stand up to your husband years before, especially for the sake of your kids. I'm so happy that you finally did do the right thing. Sometimes it just takes us a long time before hardship forces us to do what we must. For you, it had to be terrifying to confront him.

As you are now attempting to sort out what went wrong during those years, why you reacted to his sin the way you did, etc., I want to share with you some characteristics of the wife who handles her husband through appeasement.

An appeasing wife is so totally dependent upon her husband that she cannot imagine living without him and will do almost anything to keep him. Rather than receiving her value as a person from the Lord, she has always looked for it from her husband. Thus, if he is happy with her, she feels good about herself. If he is dissatisfied with her, she feels badly about herself.

When a wife like this discovers that her husband has an obsession with other women, she is devastated and often blames herself for his self-centered behavior. She does not understand that his behavior has nothing whatsoever to do with her. This problem would rear its ugly head with any addict whether he were married to the most gorgeous woman in the world or not.

As she frantically scrambles to save her marriage, she will often enter into his secret life with him. This wife may start watching pornographic movies with her husband, thinking this will help keep him satisfied at home. She hasn't a clue as to how much of a catalyst pornography is—that it fans the flames of lust he already has. While some men will have their wives perform the different sexual acts they see in the movies, others will try to persuade their wives to allow outside people into their sex lives.

For example, Richard convinced his wife, Rebecca, to do this. He sensed her lack of self worth and used this weakness to bully her into acting out his fantasies. For years they were heavily involved in the "swinging" scene. Rebecca kept thinking that he would get satisfied (or sick of it!), but he never did. The more they participated in this, the more he wanted. Did this enhance their marriage? Absolutely not!

Again, the appeasing wife will do anything she can to keep her husband. She hurts so badly, but she would rather go through degradation than to face life by herself. Then in order to cope she goes into denial along with her sex-crazed husband. She keeps making excuses for his behavior to those around them. In extreme cases, she may even have to handle all of the daily responsibilities in life because her husband is too preoccupied with sex to do anything useful around the house.

Many of these wives become addicted to drugs, alcohol or overeating as they attempt to escape the pain of their lives. I, myself, resorted to using amphetamines to avoid the pain.

Consequently, the appeasing wife panics at the thought of confronting her husband for two reasons. First, she is generally weak in that area of her life, anyway. This type of woman usually goes through life trying to avoid confrontation with *anybody*. The thought of standing up to a domineering husband is very intimidating. The other reason that confronting her husband's sin would be difficult is her fear that he would walk out on her. She is so dependent on him for everything, that she would be at a total loss if she had to live without him. Her desire to keep him blinds her to the reality that, all this considered, she would be much better off without him in her life.

Again, I am sorry for all that you have suffered through, but I am extremely happy to hear that you finally took a stand. It's a shame that your husband chose to continue in his sin, rather than try to overcome it. Let's just keep praying for him.

INTERCESSION FOR THE HUSBAND

Dear Terry,

*Y*ou asked, "How should I pray for my husband?" What a wonderful question! No doubt, it comes from the desire to see him set free of his sexual sin. I admire you for your willingness to lay down your life for Lou in this way. I would like to give you practical, everyday prayers to pray for him, but first let me share with you some principles of prayer.

Throughout Steve's period of coming out of sin, my prayerlife mainly consisted of what I will call "hope prayers," which weren't based upon a real faith and trust in God. I just sort of threw them up to heaven, hoping that God would eventually answer them.

Later, I came to realize that what matters most isn't so much the number of prayers or even their fervency necessarily, but the degree of faith they were uttered with. James said, "The effective prayer of a righteous man can accomplish much." (James 5:16) What makes a believer righteous? Over and over again in Scripture we are told that it is faith that gets God's attention. Perhaps we could state it like this: The person who prays with faith in God can accomplish much.

What is this faith in? Is it in our ability to offer up eloquent petitions to God? Is it in our ability to exercise great mental self-control, refusing to allow any doubts to lodge in our minds? Is it in our ability to pray with a lot of passion which somehow pushes a reluctant God to do something He really doesn't want to do? No, our faith is in God's character, who He is, what He's like, what we can expect from Him regardless of what we face in our lives.

Daniel, a man of great faith, prayed the following prayer:

> Alas, O Lord, the great and awesome God, who
> keeps His covenant and lovingkindness for those

who love Him and keep His commandments, we have sinned, committed iniquity, acted wickedly, and rebelled, even turning aside from Thy commandments and ordinances…To the Lord our God belong compassion and forgiveness, for we have rebelled against Him; nor have we obeyed the voice of the LORD our God, to walk in His teachings which He set before us through His servants the prophets…

So now, our God, listen to the prayer of Thy servant and to his supplications, and for Thy sake, O Lord, let Thy face shine on Thy desolate sanctuary. O my God, incline Thine ear and hear! Open Thine eyes and see our desolations and the city which is called by Thy name; for we are not presenting our supplications before Thee on account of any merits of our own, but on account of Thy great compassion. O Lord, hear! O Lord, forgive! O Lord, listen and take action! For Thine own sake, O my God, do not delay, because Thy city and Thy people are called by Thy name. (Daniel 9:4-19)

This prayer gives every indication that this man knew God intimately. He knew God to be merciful, compassionate, and quick to forgive. Therefore, it was to God's character that Daniel appealed. We should do the same whenever we pray for our husbands. When we rely upon the God of all mercy, then our faith will rise as we pray because He is a good God who desires to save. Prayers that depend on our ability to pray and convince God to do good leave us feeling defeated and empty.

What empowers our prayers is the knowledge of God's good and merciful character and a realization that the daily activity of heaven is all mercy. The atmosphere of heaven is pure, all-consuming love.

The wonderful thing about prayer that is centered in God's character is that our focus stays fixed upon Him. As we sit in His presence, His atmosphere of love invades our space. Bowed before His Majesty, we are likely to spend more time simply worshipping Him for who He is rather than fixing our eyes upon ourselves or our urgent requests. As Jesus said, "...your Father knows what you need, before you ask Him." (Matthew 6:8)

If you learn to pray like this, He will begin to change your nature to match His own. Sitting in the wonder of this God of love, mercy, and compassion will put you in the same Spirit He is in. Having the mind and heart of God for other people is the most effective way to help them. Before long, you will begin to feel the love of Christ for others, especially for your husband. The more God's love begins to shape our prayers, the more power there is in those prayers. Praying for your husband isn't a matter of convincing a reluctant God that He needs to do him a favor. It is appropriating the power of God through faith in Him to meet your husband's needs which He is already in a passion to do.

So, in light of everything I've just shared with you, allow me to make some practical suggestions concerning your daily devotions. I usually begin my time with the Lord in the Bible. Reading Scripture helps to align our minds with God's way of thinking.

It is also very important to spend some time worshipping the Lord. There is no better way to create a heavenly atmosphere. I would suggest music from Vineyard, Hillsong, or Hosanna. If these don't appeal to you, you could spend time worshipping the Lord with a hymnal or any song that leads you into a worshipful mode.

After having spent time doing these things, you are then ready to approach the throne of the Almighty with your petitions. No doubt you may have many things and people to pray for, but I would like to present some examples of words you can say to God on your husband's behalf. These phrases aren't meant to be prayed as though there is some power in the words themselves. They are only meant to provoke you to seek the Lord for your husband in faith.

Lord, there is nothing I can do to save my husband. I believe that You are good and merciful and desire to bring my husband to victory. I appeal to Your lovingkindness to help him in his great need.

Break the power of darkness over my husband's life. Break the power that sexual pleasure has over him. Make all flesh repulsive to him, except the flesh of his wife. Give him the gift of repentance. Put a hedge of protection around him. Make every illicit sexual experience he has seem empty and futile. Take away the importance sex has in his life. Diminish his need for illicit sexual behavior. Break the strong back of pride and arrogance and replace it with a spirit of humility.

Help him to make a full consecration to you, O Lord. Increase His desire for the things of God. Give him a sight of Calvary and all that the cross means. Fill him with the Spirit of holiness. Give him a hunger and thirst for righteousness. Give him the peace of God which is completeness in Christ. Meet the deepest needs of his heart, Lord. Fill the void of his heart with Yourself.

Make the mercy of God real to Him and the blood of Jesus his very life. Give him a heart of compassion for the people he takes advantage of in his mind. Give him a grateful heart, Lord. Give him the desire to lay down his life for his wife and family. Bless our marriage bed, O Lord. Make our times together fulfilling to both of us. I entrust him to You, O God, and I believe You to do everything possible to save his soul and bring him to completeness in Christ.

A FATHER'S CHASTISEMENT

Dear Lucy,

I'm so sorry to hear that your husband has run off with
another woman. News of how happy they are must be
crushing to you as everything in your life now seems to be
crashing down around you. I can understand why you feel like
God is blessing them and cursing you. They are both making
good money, going to church, and living a prosperous life,
seemingly without any troubles. All the while your life is full
of troubles. Your job hardly pays you enough to get by. The
engine in your car must be rebuilt. You feel so alone.

Lucy, has it ever occurred to you that these two may not
even know the Lord? I realize they claim to be Christians, but
their conduct is anything but Christ-like. At the very least,
they are terribly backslidden and in real delusion. Having
everything going well is not necessarily a sign of God's
blessing on one's life. In fact, in a case like this especially, it
seems more like a sign of *the lack of* God's hand being on
their lives; either that or He has simply given them over to
pursue their own lusts.

Look at your life in comparison. What I see is a sincere
believer, struggling to keep her life together and remain
faithful to the Lord in the midst of grief and adversity. I have
experienced much of this in my relationship with God—only
to discover each time that He was disciplining me for my
own good. Allow me to share the words of Solomon with
you: "My son (or daughter, in this case!), do not reject the
discipline of the LORD, or loathe His reproof, for whom the
LORD loves He reproves, even as a father, the son in whom
he delights." (Proverbs 3:11-12)

I don't know enough about this situation to make any
real judgments. But it appears to me that these two are going
their own way, without the slightest concern about what God

thinks, while you, on the other hand, are being refined in the furnace of affliction.

Don't let their outward "happiness" fool you, Lucy. Happiness based on favorable circumstances is only an inch deep. David once wrote, "Do not fret because of evildoers, be not envious toward wrongdoers." (Psalm 37:1) His son Solomon later said, "…the way of transgressors is hard." (Proverbs 13:15 KJV) One day, they will have to deal with the consequences of their actions, whether it be here on earth or standing before a holy God.

The wonderful news for you is that God loves you and is intimately and intricately involved in every aspect of your life. It may seem that He is far away during times like these, but believe me, He has never been closer. Put your husband in His hands and turn to Him for the comfort that only He can give you.

MARRIAGE IN A RUT

Dear Connie,

I believe I can give you insight into how to proceed with your husband and your marriage which appear to be "stuck." What you shared in your letter spoke volumes to me about your own personal struggles.

You began with the statement: "I have done everything I know to do to keep this marriage together and to help keep my husband in victory, all to no avail." Then in a different part of the letter, you mentioned how "dry" your walk with the Lord has been. It seemed as though these were two completely different dilemmas in your mind. But I want to help you see how closely connected they really are. First allow me to share a painful story with you.

We once had a man working with us at Pure Life who became extremely close to Steve and me. Unfortunately, the relationship soured, in large part because we foolishly allowed him to become too close to us. We failed to maintain the boundaries that come when proper spiritual authority has been established.

Ted did just about everything right, most of the time, but the time came when Steve and I had to dismiss him from his position on staff at PLM. From the perspective of someone on the outside it may have seemed that we were wrong in our decision. Everyone loved and respected Ted because outwardly he had a very pleasant disposition. But there was something going on in his heart that only those closest to him could detect: it was an unsubmissive attitude and an unwillingness to repent.

Ted had a tremendous ability to discern problems in the lives of others. The Lord was able to use this gift to help many men whom he counseled. Over the years that the three of us worked together, Ted quietly became lifted up in pride.

He was acutely aware of Steve's faults, which tend to stand out glaringly. He demanded that Steve walk near perfection, and was quick to confront him if he didn't but was downright indignant if we tried to point out any error in his life. Steve, being extremely aware of his own weaknesses, would always humble himself to Ted and accept correction. The desire to be Christ-like was so strong in him that he would accept reproof from just about anybody.

Gradually, Ted became, in his mind, Steve's counselor. This was not his place, and Steve was wrong to allow him that much authority, even if he was trying to be humble. The bottom line was that Ted became so aware of Steve's faults, that he became extremely self-righteous and neglected to examine his own heart. So eventually when Steve had to confront him, he became furious. At that point, we had no choice but to let him go.

We often see this same attitude in the wives we counsel. A wife can easily become so consumed with her husband's sin that she won't allow God to examine her own heart. All she sees is his failings, his faults, his shortcomings. She is completely blinded to the log in her own eye. Meanwhile, the sincere husband humbles himself before God, accepts His correction, and matures as a Christian. Unfortunately, the wife stays stagnant, full of self-righteousness and pride. In other words, he grows and she remains spiritually immature.

One wise pastor we know once said, "Most people either come out of a life of deep sin or out of a life of deep self-righteousness." That is so true.

Connie, please don't allow pride to destroy you as it did Ted. Humble yourself before God and invite Him to bring correction into your life, to show you areas in your own life that aren't pleasing to Him. As you do, you will become sweeter, more Christ-like, and a much greater support to your husband. You can't keep your husband in victory, as you stated, but you can be a blessing and an encouragement to him along the way. In the meantime, I suspect that you will find the spiritual dryness disappearing and your marriage climbing out of the rut!

DEALING WITH FEAR

Dear Alice,

Thank you for sharing your struggles with me. I must admit that it is so difficult to try to help through letters. There is simply not enough time to cover everything that needs to be addressed. However, I would like to express some things regarding your fear, which seems to dominate your life more than anything else.

I know what it's like to be paralyzed and controlled by fear; it held me in its icy grip for many years. The reason I couldn't get free of it was that my perceptions about it were faulty. I became so accustomed to living in fear that I was convinced that I had a right to be fearful. I saw myself as being the helpless victim of an overwhelming feeling I could not control. Because I embraced the role of the victim, I expected people to feel sorry for me.

One of my biggest fears was that of getting in a car wreck. Whenever Steve and I would drive somewhere, I would continually lecture him about his driving: "slow down," "be careful," "watch out," and so on. One day, a number of years ago, I made one of my comments as we were driving down the road. To my utter astonishment, he sharply rebuked me about it.

"Do you know how selfish you're being? All you're concerned about is preserving your own life!" He went on to describe how it affected him to have me constantly criticizing and trying to control his driving. I reacted a little defensively at first but quickly backed down, knowing that what he was saying was true, and more than that, I knew that it was from the Lord for me.

My eyes were opened to the fact that I was being completely selfish. My fears were totally unwarranted. There was nothing reckless about Steve's driving; I was simply allowing myself to focus on the worst possible scenarios.

That day, I began to see things in a different light. The Lord showed me that fear is based in a lack of trust in Him, and it is therefore sinful. Believe it or not, that was wonderful news! Why? I was no longer a helpless victim with no hope of ever overcoming my fears. Since it was sin I had a way out. I could now repent of being fearful and ask the Lord to help me overcome it. With repentance as a starting point, the Lord was now able to demonstrate His faithfulness and help me.

We all tend to be fearful to some degree, and one of the greatest sources of fear, for women, has to do with their marriages. We tend to worry about relationships more than men do. Relationships mean everything to us. Our lives revolve around our families, and anything that threatens those relationships can quickly become a source of much anxiety.

Most chronic worriers don't look for help from the Lord about their worrying because unfortunately they are very comfortable with it. They've always dealt with their problems that way. *It takes less effort to sit and fret than to kneel and pray.* When we are imprisoned by fear, we are relying on our own thinking to handle our problems instead of turning our cares over to the One who can help us.

The root of fear is self-preservation and self-centeredness, being preoccupied with one's own life. Often the woman who is worried about a relationship is really only concerned about herself.* It is not uncommon to counsel with a wife who isn't too concerned about her husband's needs but only how his actions—his problem—will affect her. When confronted about this, the wife who does love her family tends to get defensive and even resentful. But it's true nonetheless.

---

* I don't mean to infer it is some evil thing for a wife to be concerned about her marriage. My point is simply that when that concern becomes an overwhelming fear, something is amiss.

The truth of the matter is fear doesn't produce anything good whatsoever. It excludes God from the picture and makes you rely on your own ability to think out a solution. It keeps you stuck in yourself and away from the Lord. It brings nothing but torment, and the more you give over to fearful imaginations, the more tormented and selfish you will become. You will only experience a sense of peace when things go exactly the way you want them to go.

How differently did the apostle Paul think. The reason fear didn't control his mind, even though he experienced fearful circumstances, was because his life was consumed with the well-being of others. From Macedonia, the place of numerous beatings and much suffering, he wrote: "Therefore we do not lose heart, but though our outer man is decaying, yet our inner man is being renewed day by day." (II Corinthians 4:16) There was no place for fear in Paul's life because he was committed to seeing and meeting the needs of others.

Turn to God, Alice. Repent of the selfishness that keeps fear alive in your heart. Start becoming involved in the lives of others. Then watch and see what the Lord will do for you. Remember: Perfect love (devotion to others) casts out fear. (I John 4:18)

THE FAILING HUSBAND

Dear Veronica,

Although it may be difficult for you to see it now, you are blessed to have Stan for a husband—struggles and all! I say this because he is earnestly pursuing God and refuses to give up.

You asked, "How can such a good husband and father, who spends quality time with the Lord everyday, continue to struggle with something so filthy as pornography?"

Stan is a sinner, like all of us, who has grown up in a culture in which sexual perversion has almost become the norm. From childhood men are bombarded with the message that having sex is the ultimate form of pleasure and pleasure is the reason for life. I'm not at all shocked that so many men are addicted to pornography in America today—even Christian men (cf., letter to Miriam).

Because your husband is doing all of the right things—being open with you, repenting, spending time with the Lord each day, and staying accountable—there is no need to worry or fear that your marriage will take a turn for the worse. No doubt, it will take some time before total victory is his. You must be patient with him as he outgrows his obsession with sex. His occasional slips are painful setbacks, but somehow the Lord is faithful to use them for good in the life of a sincere believer. Stan has demonstrated that he wants to break free from sexual sin and that he wants the Lord. So, there is a lot of hope for the two of you!

I can remember when Steve got serious about overcoming his sin. It really hurt whenever he gave over to some temptation, but all along those failures were actually working in our favor. Each time he blew it, his hatred for his sin deepened, and he learned how to walk in daily repentance. Eventually, he reached a point where he began to count the cost and make a conscious choice to resist the temptations he faced.

It sounds like Stan is in the same place Steve was in just before he really came into victory. Be encouraged! Stan is a fighter and by God's grace he will make it!

THE NEGLECTED WIFE

Dear Tammy,

The first thing you asked in your letter to me was whether Steve would compliment me or show me affection when he was still in his sexual sin. I must infer by that question, you are feeling neglected by your husband—that he is not making you feel accepted and loved. This is fairly typical for a woman married to a man struggling with sexual sin.

You must understand what happens to a man who has gotten involved with pornography. It is like a poison that gets into his system. It corrupts the way he views sex, women, and personal relationships. To make matters worse, it is extremely addictive, keeping the man coming back for more, again and again. Every new trip to the porn shop further deepens the corruption of his heart.

Another thing to understand is that many men are not affectionate by nature. They can be, when they first meet a girl they are falling in love with, but typically, as soon as the honeymoon is over, they settle into a daily life where affection isn't a top priority for them. For most men, they are content to know that their wives are there. Apart from the effects of sexual sin, most husbands need to be taught how to love their wives, how to express affection, how to compliment, and how to caress. Affection simply does not come naturally to some men.

Another thing that can make the situation even worse, is when the husband has been raised in a home where love has been poorly or inappropriately expressed. This was the case with my husband, who was never told by his parents that he was loved. On the other hand, I grew up in a home where we kids knew we were loved. My parents had their faults and failed us in some ways, but it was always evident that they loved each other and they loved us. This kind of upbringing establishes something in a person's heart that those without it lack.

As I mentioned before, the man who becomes involved with illicit sexual activity, even if it is only occasionally viewing pornography, becomes deeply affected in many areas of his life by it. It distorts his perspectives on sexuality, women, marriage, and even life itself. In some unexplainable way, it creates a barrier between the man and his loved ones. He becomes aloof and superficial. He shies away from meaningful conversations. He has a secret fantasy life going on inside that nobody knows about. His obsession with the fantasy life causes him to drift outside of the realm of reality. The important things of life: love, friendships, God, etc., lose their appeal. For him, life revolves around his secret world of fantasy and pleasure. It's not that he is purposely being unloving; it is simply part of the package that comes with an addiction to pornography. In some ways he becomes dead emotionally.

All of this, of course, is devastating to those who love him and are looking to him for affection and support. But unfortunately, he simply doesn't have it to give. Until he has broken free of the influences of pornography, he can't be expected to react normally to his loved ones.

There's one other aspect to all of this I want to mention to you. Your husband's attraction to seeing nude women doesn't mean that there is something wrong with you. The problem is completely with him—in *his* heart. We have often told wives that it wouldn't matter if they looked like Marilyn Monroe. A man addicted to pornography is simply going to be attracted to other women. In one sense, this can alleviate a lot of the pressure you have placed on yourself to try to look prettier, sexier, and so on. I'm not suggesting that you should let yourself go, but the root of your husband's obsession is in his heart, not in your looks.

The best thing you can do to attract your husband, is to allow the Lord to change you into His image. You have heard it said that beauty is only skin deep, but there is a beauty that God can clothe you with that begins on the inside and transforms the way you look to all who see you. It isn't the sort of sexiness that attracts the carnal attention of men, but a spiritual beauty that emanates from your entire person.

Having said all this, I encourage you to be patient with your husband as he fights his way out of this deep pit, realizing that for awhile you won't be able to look to him for a lot of emotional support. If you lower your expectations, in this area, you will be less disappointed. Turn to God and allow Him to change you from the inside. And remember: God is working in both of your lives.

THE POLICE WIFE

Dear Kelly,

*Y*ou gave me a wealth of information in your letter concerning your efforts to help your husband overcome his sexual sin. I think I can help you. You mentioned, "I do everything I can to help him, but he just keeps blowing it. I monitor his money and his time. I hold him accountable for his actions. I ask him every night how he did that day. I confront him regularly about his sin," and so forth.

Let's take a close look at what you said. Do you see the one word that keeps recurring? I, I, I! Over and over again you stress what *you* are doing to help your husband. I must ask you: where is God in all of this?

Based upon what you have shared with me so far, you strike me as being the sort of person who likes to be in control of the circumstances in her life. Your husband's struggle with lust and masturbation is both extremely disconcerting and quite a challenge for you because you can't seem to get him to do what he's supposed to do.

I'm pretty sure that you are even more involved in his battle to overcome than what you shared in your letter. How often do you make cutting remarks about his failures? How often do you badger or criticize him? Do you ever try to shame Ben in front of others about his sin? How would Ben describe your efforts to support him?

I realize that you have been deeply hurt by his interest in other women, and I don't want to minimize your pain in any way. I only want to help you better deal with it. What you will have to face, Kelly, is that you cannot make your husband to do the right thing. You can't talk him into it; you can't shame him into it; you can't police him into it; and you can't threaten him into it. However, what you *can* do is begin learning the secret of how to entrust him into the hands of the Lord.

After all, only God can change his heart.

My dear sister, if you ever learn how to harness that zeal, in a constructive way, hell will begin to tremble! I want to encourage you to begin biting your tongue. Every time you feel the need to correct or confront your husband, stifle the words and immediately begin praying for him. Your badgering will only help to keep your husband stuck where he is.

Learn to turn to God in your pain rather than trying to solve the problem through fleshly means. The Lord is very motivated in His desire to help your husband. But what He needs is someone who is willing to stand in the gap for Ben. Channel that energy to oversee your husband's life in a positive direction by bearing him to God daily and then stand back and watch the hand of the Lord work on your behalf!

RECONCILIATION

Dear Sonja,

$\mathscr{G}$ etting back together after a one-year separation must be both quite exciting and yet scary. I'm glad to hear that your pastor is involved and has been very supportive in your situation. Thank you for allowing me to add my insights on how to follow through with reconciliation.

First, before taking the big step forward there should be definite progress in your husband's life that is both visible and measurable. For instance, during your occasional visits together does he still get impatient and angry? Does he demand that things go his way? Do you get the sense that he is putting on a show for you but is someone entirely different when nobody is looking? I know it may seem silly, but the answers to these questions are good indicators that he has or has not dealt with some basic issues. If he is still struggling in these areas, he probably hasn't dealt with the deeper issues.

Another place to look to for a sign of how he is doing is his "accountability partner." Does he have someone to whom he holds himself accountable? Have you asked for this man's impressions about how Chris is doing? I encourage you to first verify his progress. Depending on the outcome, it might be wise to put off reconciliation until he has established closer accountability with someone you can trust. Ask your pastor for his input in this as well. If your husband shows an unwillingness to open up to someone else, then I would definitely back off on any immediate plans for reconciliation. An unwillingness to humble oneself to another is a glaring red flag that things aren't right.

I imagine that he is anxious for the two of you to get back together, but is he considerate of your timetable and feelings? Or, has he been pushy and impatient? A sign of true repentance is that he is willing to do whatever it takes to make things right with you. Don't allow him to pressure you into his timetable.

Does he seem to be hungry for the Lord? By this I mean is he in the Word of God voluntarily? Does he spend time in prayer without being coerced? Does he go to church as often as possible? While you can't expect perfection, you can insist that he demonstrates a genuine desire for this kind of life. If you have to push him into living the Christian life, what does that say about him?

Before you officially end the separation, it is important that you both lay out some ground rules about what is to be expected by both parties. He should be involved in some type of structured Bible study. He should have his prayer time well established. He should continue meeting with his accountability partner and also, occasionally, touch bases with your pastor. I would even suggest you put all of your expectations down in writing, along with a clause that states if he fails to maintain this lifestyle, then he agrees to another separation until such time that he again proves his faithfulness.

Be prepared to hit some low spots. Don't panic when they come. Remember, you are not looking for perfection from him, only a sincere willingness to grow, mature, and overcome.

In a sense, the pressure is on your husband to win you back. It is right that it is so. You must walk the fine line between being an encouragement to him, even when he blows it, and standing strong in your expectations of his faithfulness. Even though he has done well out there on his own, he may get tempted to slack off a little once the pressure is off. Try to be patient, but at the same time hold him accountable.

Work to foster in the children an attitude of acceptance and love for their father. I'm sure it's already there, but some children have some difficulty in this adjustment period. It's not harmful to encourage such acceptance; it is Christ-like.

It would also be a very good thing for the two of you to set aside one night out of the week where you can be alone. If you aren't yet quite ready to get back together, now is the time to initiate this practice. Go out on dates, but don't be intimate with him until you are once again living as husband and wife! This weekly time together should be something very special for both of you. Do your best to make it special for him; it will be a real source of encouragement to him.

It sounds as though the two of you are well on your way to a wonderful reconciliation. Don't be afraid to expect the best!

THE AGGRAVATED WIFE

Dear Penny,

I believe I can sum up the source of your frustrations and aggravations in one word: ingratitude. Other people are not your problem, Penny. It's the spirit you are in. Others can provoke us, but we must choose to respond the right way. Good or bad, only what is in us will come out.

Some of the things you expressed in your letter, gave me a picture of who you are as a person—the real you when no one is looking. My guess is that you tend to be negative and critical more often than not. You scrutinize every detail. You are a faultfinder always looking for the worst in others. This makes you frustrated with others when they don't act "the way they're supposed to."

These characteristics don't make you a monster. God has a way out of it for you. You are not trapped. You can choose to repent of being unmerciful, critical, and ungrateful. I want to challenge you to sit down and repent to the Lord for the way you have treated others in your heart. You certainly haven't loved them the way the Lord has loved you. Next, you should go to your husband and repent to him for the way you have treated him.

Once you have done this, you are ready to go to the next step: cultivating an attitude of gratitude. God has done so much for you, Penny. Start by making a list of fifty things the Lord has done for you for which you are grateful. The following week, make a list of fifty things for which you are grateful about in your husband. The next week, write out fifty things for which you are grateful about in your life. Then do the same with your job, your home, your boss, your family, your pastor, your neighbors, etc. If you will begin to do this regularly, it will help to put you into the correct mindset concerning life.

If you will do these things, Penny, you will be amazed at how quickly you change from being (forgive me for saying it!) an old Scrooge to someone whom people want to be around. Being grateful is the key!

THE LOVE LIFE

Dear Paula,

I n answer to your question, "Why doesn't my husband love me?" I would like to put forth the idea that he does love you, it's just not a godly love. Allow me to explain. There are four Greek words which describe what we sum up in the one English word *love: phileo, storge, agape* and *eros.* I will try to say some things about each in relation to your marriage.

The word *phileo* means "brotherly love." It is the sense of friendship that develops between two people which must be the basis for the marriage relationship. Good marriages begin with good friendships.

Storge is the marital glue which binds a couple together more closely as the years go by. It is a sense of commitment which deepens as a couple experiences life together. It produces an abiding trust which allows them to be open and vulnerable to each other. This sense of affection, one for the other, takes time to develop, and it is the basis for the statement often made by a husband who has enjoyed a good relationship over the years: "I love her more than ever!"

While *phileo, storge* and *eros* are emotions which are generated from within the human soul, *agape* comes from God. In fact, the Bible tells us that "God is *agape.*" (I John 4:8) This type of love is divine because it is utterly selfless and only considers the other person's well being. A person who is filled with Jesus is subsequently filled with His love for others. It is *agape* love which provokes a godly woman to patiently bear with and intercede for an unlovable husband. Only God can love a person in this way, but mature Christians know how to allow Him to love others through them.

I have saved *eros* for last because it seems that this has been the primary affection upon which your marriage has been based. I don't mean to imply that there aren't traces of the others in varying degrees, but simply that this one seems to be predominant.

Before I talk about your relationship, allow me to say some things about this natural drive. *Eros* is erotic love—operating in the pleasure principle only. It has its place in the godliest of marriages, but left unbalanced by the other three "loves," you end up with a selfish arrangement in which one, if not both, loves the other simply for what he or she gets out of the relationship. Author Kay Arthur says the following about it:

> "Though eros is directed towards another, it actually has self in mind. For example, ' I love you because you make me happy.'
>
> "The foundation of this type of love is some characteristic in the other person which pleases you. If the characteristic would cease to exist, the reason for the love would be gone, the result being, 'I don't love you anymore.'
>
> "Eros looks for what it can receive. If it does give, it gives in order to receive. If it fails to get what it wants or expects, bitterness or resentment could develop...
>
> "The philosophy of eros is that being loved depends on being attractive in some way to another person. Because of this dependency, eros would be considered a conditional type of love."*

This seems to sum up your relationship with Carl. By your own admission, you were attracted to him in the beginning because of his looks. Likewise, it seems that he was attracted to your looks as well. From your first date you began having sex together. Your sex life started off "great" and has only

---

* Kay Arthur, *Marriage Without Regrets*, Precept Ministries, Chattanooga, TN.

gotten better. Even after the two of you came to the Lord and got married, the relationship seemed to find its strength in the bedroom.

Now, five years later, you feel like the relationship is empty. The emptiness you feel is the neglect on both of your parts of initiating and fostering the other three types of love in your home.

Having a "great" sex life is a good thing. Even though Carl continues to struggle with lust and pornography, I suspect the fulfillment he receives at home has had a lot to do with why he hasn't been unfaithful to you. Now it's time for you both to put forth a more diligent effort at learning to be unselfish in your relationship. You be the initiator, Paula. Just begin doing little acts of kindness to him. He probably won't even notice it at first, let alone reciprocate. But give him time. If you just keep showing him unselfish love, and not make the mistake of telling him about it, or worse, getting mad because he doesn't show enough appreciation, in time he will probably respond.

Also, more importantly, start a life of real intercession for your husband. There is nothing that creates and fosters *agape* love like prayer. Those prayers transform you into a vessel of God's love, and helps the Lord accomplish the work in your husband He wishes to accomplish.

THE RELENTLESS WIFE

Dear Margaret,

I must say that I am somewhat shocked to hear that Jeff
filed for divorce. I know our last meeting with you was very
hard. Steve would not allow the counseling to continue
because it didn't seem as though you were open.

Perhaps, now that Jeff is gone, you will be more open to
what we have been trying to say to you all along. From the
first time we counseled you, we sort of sensed that you saw
yourself as a victim of Jeff's perversity. There is some truth
to that, of course, since he was involved in sexual sin behind
your back.

However, one major obstacle we found to be detrimental
to Jeff's progress was your negative, unmerciful attitude
toward him. You demanded that he walk a straight line of
perfection, unwilling to show patience or be supportive and
loving to him. It was virtually impossible for him to live up to
your high expectations. As we attempted to counsel him and
show him the way out, time and time again we felt as though
our efforts to help him were being thwarted at home by your
cynicism and accusations.

Another thing that was regrettable was your decision not
to have sex with him. It underscored your unwillingness to
believe in him.

Whenever I tried to discuss these things with you in our
counseling sessions, the conversation would without fail shift
from talking about your life to listing all of the offenses Jeff
had committed that week. Also, not satisfied with his failures,
you continually brought unsubstantiated accusations against
him. You were bent on building a case against your husband
and became so paranoid that we were unable to reason with
you.

The fact of the matter was that, although Jeff once had

a problem with pornography, he had repented of it. He admitted that he still struggled with looking at women in public and came to us for help—voluntarily! But you treated him with the severity due a husband who is going out with prostitutes and has no intentions of changing one bit. As a result he grew discouraged and felt as though he could never meet your demands. Yes, he was a failure in some areas, but you treated him as though he were a loser who would never get it together. You cannot treat a man that way and expect him to stay.

I feel so bad for you, Margaret, not only because your heart is broken over this divorce, but mostly because it sounds like you still think of yourself as the only victim in this marriage. The sad fact is that due to your bitterness and resentment you have chosen a path of misery and unhappiness which will remain unaltered until you repent. It seems as though the likelihood of your coming to repentance is a million miles from your thoughts, though.

I must admit that I am puzzled over your desire to see the marriage restored. What is there to restore? If Jeff is "the same ole creep" he ever was, why would you want to go back with him?

I do not believe you can be restored to Jeff until you are first restored to God. That will only happen when you come to realize that you, too, are a sinner in desperate need of the grace of God. When you get a real sight of Calvary, the place where the Innocent One laid down His life for your sins, then you will be ready to fall to your knees humbled and broken before the Lord.

Jesus once told the story of two men who went to the temple to pray. One saw himself as a filthy sinner, unworthy even to look up to God. The other saw himself as someone walking in tremendous spirituality, far beyond others around him. Jesus said that only one of these men left the temple

justified in the sight of God. Margaret, your future with
God depends upon which of these two attitudes you take
into God's throne room. If you humble yourself and repent,
I'm sure that there is not only hope for this marriage to be
restored, but a bright hope for your future happiness as well.

THE UNREPENTANT HUSBAND

Dear Sue,

Thanks for your note. I appreciate your openness and
honesty. It's so hard to know what to say to someone who has
endured so much from a husband who has repeated the same
behavior over and over again.

You have gone through the many stages of grief that
a wife goes through when dealing with a husband who is a
sexual addict. And I will admit that most women would not
put up with what you have had to deal with. It would be easy
to grow angry and very bitter. But God, who specializes in
heart surgery, will use His razor sharp scalpel to remove from
your heart any evidence of cancer because of His great love
for you. He will not allow bitterness to eat away your soul as
long as you keep turning to Him.

I cannot tell you what I would do in your situation, Sue.
The recent discovery of your husband's dabbling in bestiality
does shed new light on the situation and further complicates
things. It is a very frightening line that your husband has
crossed. It is good that he has at least admitted it rather than
being caught in the very act. But hasn't that always been his
pattern? It is very unusual that a man will be honest about
his sin if he isn't sincere about getting help, but Gil has had a
track record of feeling conviction, confessing with his mouth,
but remaining committed to it in his heart.

True repentance is the key to breaking the cycle. What good
is it to be honest if you don't repent? None, whatsoever! I tend
to think that admitting his sin gives Gil some kind of temporary
relief from the tremendous guilt he feels. Perhaps in some
twisted way he convinces himself that he is sincere in his efforts
because he voluntarily tells on himself. But true repentance
yields real fruit which translates into changed behavior that is
observable. However, this never seems to happen for him.

I fear that Gil may be headed for or perhaps has already crossed the point where God will give him completely over to his degrading passions. If that has truly happened, then he has placed himself beyond the reach of the Holy Spirit's conviction. Another possibility is that Gil has never experienced a true conversion to Christ. He may have simply learned how to play the part of Christianity outwardly without ever having truly received a regenerated heart. That would certainly explain the lack of true repentance.

I am convinced that one of Gil's biggest hindrances has been that he is a "nice guy" which makes it easy for him to convince himself that he is godly. People with pleasant natures are very susceptible to this kind of delusion.

As far as whether or not you should separate from him, I strongly encourage you to do so for several reasons. You must take into account how his sin could be affecting the children. They have already discovered one of his magazines. Furthermore, it is very likely that all kinds of spirits are abiding in your home because of his perversions. Sin like this tends to have far-reaching implications. Your husband is probably like most men in sexual sin who think that their behavior doesn't affect others, but that is certainly not true. Your pastor can help you think through some of the other implications of such a decision.

Gil's lack of concern about the consequences of his behavior somewhat amazes me. I realize that you haven't always handled everything perfectly, but you have stuck it out with him. Perhaps a separation is just the kind of shaking he needs at this point. Our prayers are with you.

THE ADULTEROUS WIFE

Dear Stacey,

Do you really believe it would help your marriage (or you)
to do to your husband what he has done to you? Why haven't
you done it yet? I tend to think that you are just very hurt
right now and aren't really that serious about committing
adultery.

I can remember so well being twenty-two years old,
hurting and broken-hearted. I was very vulnerable because
I wasn't turning to the Lord for my comfort and help. Of
course, the devil was only too happy to supply an alternative
source of comfort, which came in the form of a man who
appeared to be concerned about me and full of compassion.
Within minutes of meeting me, this man figured out how
naive and vulnerable I was. I didn't realize it at the time, but
I was a walking target for someone like him. Foolishly, I
allowed my emotions to run away with me. Before I knew
what had happened, I was whisked away in a new relationship
that seemed to promise the world.

What I really needed at that time was a godly Christian
woman who could sit me down and talk some sense into me.
Unfortunately, I made many unwise decisions. Oh, if I could
only share with you how deeply I have regretted things I've
done down through the years!

Stacey, you too, are very vulnerable right now. If you don't
turn to the Lord, the devil will set you up just like he did to
me years ago. Some guy, posing as Prince Charming, will
suddenly appear in your life. What you won't realize is how
blinded you are by your own pain. You will miss the little red
flags that should warn you as to what this guy is really like.
You will fall right into the trap and find your life in a much
bigger mess than ever before.

Trying to find relief through some carnal method will

only lead to more problems and heartaches. You will find yourself caught in a vicious cycle of sin, shame and fear that will become increasingly more difficult to escape. Believe it or not, you are at a crossroad right now. The wrong decision could literally ruin the rest of your life.

What I would suggest to you, now, is to try to calm yourself down. Why not spend some time meditating in the Psalms? I know it doesn't seem as though it would be any help to your situation, but it will put you into the mindset of the Lord. The praise and adoration of the Lord conveyed in the Psalms can really help to bring you into an atmosphere of peace and comfort.

Next, try to make an appointment with either your pastor or his wife. It would do you a lot of good to have someone like that intimately involved in your life right now. I realize it may be embarrassing to confess your struggles, but they will understand. More importantly, it will bring your temptations out into the light where mature Christians will be able to help you to deal with and overcome them.

Stacey, what you are experiencing right now is the worst part of it. This situation, as black as it may seem, will get better if you make the right decisions. One day you will look back on this time and thank the Lord for helping you through it. We will pray that God will supply you with the needed strength to get through this painful and difficult time.

MY SEXUAL NEEDS

Dear Darlene,

You are right; there are no easy answers to your problem. Your husband's lack of interest in you sexually makes his interest in pornography all the harder to handle emotionally.

It is very difficult for me not to get emotional and impassioned over this subject when I consider the extreme selfishness of men who expect sex on demand, unconcerned about meeting the needs of their wives. Men like this usually think that sex is meant just for them.

Many men don't realize that women have needs which are just as real as theirs. It may be true that a woman doesn't have the hormonal build-up that a man has, however, a woman's emotional needs, which require some degree of real intimacy, more than makes up for the other. You know, only too well, how you begin to feel rejected inside when your husband neglects you after he has reached fulfillment.

I have a friend who has dealt with this very problem for a long time. Sue has been married to Jimmy for twelve years, but figures in the last eleven years, they have been intimate only about a dozen times. Jimmy's struggle has been with homosexuality, which explains some of his problems. Other women suffer, as you do, with a husband who has become addicted to pornography and masturbation to the point where sex with their spouse is nearly impossible. Whatever the reason, the wife is the one who suffers.

Sue's reaction to the neglect would vacillate between tolerance and acceptance to anger and resentment. One of the unfortunate consequences of Jimmy's lack of concern for her was that their relationship never deepened beyond a superficial level. When a person is truly intimate and vulnerable to another there are no secrets and no holding back. It was the distance between the two that bothered Sue the most.

Unfortunately, Sue wouldn't really turn to the Lord for help. She would make feeble attempts at praying and asking for help, but her need for Jimmy's attention became her all-consuming passion to the point where her walk with the Lord just dried up.

In this state of mind, it wasn't hard for Sue to justify her increasing problem with masturbation. Whenever a person masturbates, sexual fantasy is involved. Little by little, Sue's heart became blackened with lust. It wasn't that she walked around lusting over men; it was more subtle than that. It was more a fantasy of romance that dominated her heart, encouraged in part by her ever-increasing involvement in reading romance novels and watching soap operas. It usually only became sexual fantasy when she was masturbating.

These romantic fantasies further increased the distance between her and Jimmy because they were a constant reminder of his failure as a husband. She noticed that the more involved she became in the novels and soaps, the more resentful she felt toward him.

The Lord began dealing with Sue's heart. Heavy conviction would come upon her when she would masturbate and even when she would watch the soap operas. The conviction of the Holy Spirit quietly increased until one morning she woke up and knew that she had to repent. The question that formed in her mind was, "How is what I'm doing in my heart any different than what Jimmy is doing?" This question jolted her into reality. She tearfully turned to the Lord that morning in great repentance. The basis of her brokenness was that she was wrong and needed God. She decided she was going to obey and trust the Lord no matter what Jimmy did.

The first thing she did was to get rid of the romance novels. Boxes of them went into the trash. She then volunteered to spend her afternoons at the church daycare center. Thus she not only severed the temptation to watch soap operas, but also got involved in helping others. She spent every morning studying the Word of God, which in her new-found brokenness, came alive to her. For her, she found doing inductive studies (produced by Precept Ministries) helped restore her lost passion for the Scriptures. A solid prayer time became a part of her routine, as well. Almost overnight Sue became a different person.

This freshness in the Lord also had a real impact on her relationship with Jimmy. Even though he still wasn't meeting her needs, she repented of her resentment toward him. This helped to bridge the gap that had grown between them over the years. With this repentance came an end to the complaining spirit she had nurtured about him. As Jesus became more real to her, the problems of her marriage gradually diminished in her mind. The more focused she became on the Lord, the more His power to work on her behalf became real to her. This helped her to be more supportive and understanding of Jimmy's struggles.

Recently, I received a glowing report from her. It seems that several weeks after Sue had her experience with God, Jimmy had his own. "I am married to a new man," she wrote. "He treats me like a princess, and we make love on a regular basis. We are definitely having our first, real honeymoon."

What brought about the change? Repentance, on both of their parts. A wife in this situation can't turn to God as some sort of formula to get her husband to do what she wants him to do. She must come to the realization that her life has been displeasing to God and desire to get right with Him. There are no guarantees that the husband will do the right thing just because she did. However, there are two certainties. First, if a wife who has gotten in this kind of spirit repents, she will find the wonderful presence of Jesus filling her life. Her problems will diminish in His awesome presence. Second, as she gets right with God, it will enable Him to work on her behalf with her husband in a much greater way. Again, there are no guarantees, but the chances of him repenting are greatly increased.

Jesus is your husband, Darlene, and He knows your needs. I know there are many who consider this kind of teaching to be unrealistic or perhaps, even naive. All I can say is that perspective comes from human logic. God's power to do good, on behalf of the one who comes to Him, is far greater than our problems. However, I have found that many women simply don't have that degree of trust in the Lord and are unwilling to put their faith in Him. My testimony to you, is that when a wife really turns to God in trust, He never fails or disappoints her.

THE CHILD MOLESTER

Dear Ericka,

I am so sorry to hear about your daughter. What could be worse for a wife to deal with, than for her husband to molest one of her children? I appreciated the sincerity of your questions about whether you should stick it out with him or just divorce him. In one sense, it is good that he is going to be in prison for a couple of years: this will give you some time to really seek the mind of the Lord on this.

Please refer to the letters I have written to Sonja and Pam about reconciliation and looking for fruits of repentance. What I want to talk to you about are some of the things you will face being married to a child molester.

Once he is released from prison and allowed to move back in with you (this usually doesn't occur upon prison release, but after he has completed the state's sexual offender program while out on his own), you must keep in mind that he will be a registered sex offender for the rest of his life. This community safeguard makes it more difficult for the man (and his family) who is truly trying to change. It is a stigma that he will bear for some time.

Another thing to consider is that, at some point, he will have to prove by his actions that he can be trusted. With an adulterer, this isn't such a problem, but one "slip" from a molester bears tragic consequences. This is a serious issue for you to consider as a mother.

I am not implying that God can't utterly change a person's heart. We have seen the vilest offenders completely broken and changed by the Lord. But in all sincerity, I feel that I must also inform you that we haven't had a good success rate with child molesters. Most psychologists insist that it isn't possible for a molester to change. We know from experience that God can do the impossible if a man truly repents. The problem we have found is that, in the case of most offenders, their sin has taken them to such extremes of delusion and insanity that they are no longer able to respond to the conviction of the Holy Spirit. And so, they are driven to repeat their offenses despite the consequences—life behind bars.

By and large, child molesters are notorious blameshifters. I suppose they have a difficult time accepting the responsibility for their despicable actions. But moreover, sin deceives the heart, and sin of this depth and magnitude brings with it a corresponding depth of delusion. If you find your husband blame shifting or justifying his actions, you can be sure he hasn't truly repented of his behavior.

Another common problem associated with a man molesting his step-daughter is that sometimes the mother struggles with resentment toward her daughter. She may question (especially if the husband has inferred this) how much of it was provoked in some way by her daughter. It has been our experience that (especially in the case of a younger girl) this is rarely the case. Sometimes however, a young teenage girl will attempt to seduce her step-father. But this too is extremely rare, unless she has already been sexually promiscuous. More typical cases of molestation or incest involve the step-daughter seeking affection from her new daddy, who—in his warped thinking—misreads this as a sexual invitation.

Just be aware that you may experience a tremendous struggle inside toward your daughter. If you know that she has been promiscuous in the past and suspect that she in some way intentionally incited your husband's passions, you must deal with her from that standpoint. (This in no way alleviates your husband's responsibility who, being the adult, should have known better. It does make it a little more understandable, however.)

Unless you have absolute proof, you should give her

every benefit of the doubt that she was innocent in the whole affair. I know that this entire ordeal has been extremely painful to you, but please, show all the sensitivity and compassion toward her that you can. She has been violated and emotionally damaged. The one thing that would make it unbearable is to sense any resentment from you or to be reminded that the home has been split up because of her. Also, if your daughter feels that you are bent on getting back together with him regardless of her feelings, she will lose her trust in you as well. It might be difficult for her to understand why you would want to get back together with someone who has hurt her so much. I'm not suggesting that you cater to her every whim and demand, only that you take her feelings into consideration.

We dealt with one family where the husband became obsessed with his step-daughter to the point of peeking in her windows. He received help from us, as did the wife. She, too, struggled with resentment toward her daughter, but upon seeing it for what it was, was able to repent before it became a problem between the two of them. When his graduation from our live-in program drew near, she began talking to her daughter about her husband coming home. Her daughter was very fearful, but this woman assured her that she would not tolerate any more incidents from her husband. This, along with the help she received from a biblical counselor, seemed to reassure her. The last we heard, the family was doing well.

Whether she is guilty or not, it is important that your daughter receives counseling immediately. She needs to be able to work through all of the conflicting emotions and feelings that will arise from this. If she isn't given the opportunity to do this, be assured that the devil will use it to twist her mind and wreak further havoc in her life.

The sense I got from your letter, Ericka, was that you are very committed to your husband and that you just want to do the right thing. From the few things you mentioned about him, you seem convinced that he has truly repented. Be sure to seek the mind of the Lord, consider your daughter's feelings, and be very careful how you handle things. May God bless your efforts as you pursue healing for yourself and your family.

ACCOUNTABILITY

Dear Deanna,

I will offer you some helpful guidelines for holding your husband accountable, but are you sure you can handle it? If he tells you that he bought a magazine after work and masturbated, how will you react? If he tells you he is having a struggle with a girl at his job, what will you do? If he tells you he is having homosexual fantasies, will you still respect him? Once he begins baring his soul, you can expect the unexpected.

It has been our experience that it is better for the wife to take a limited role in her husband's accountability. The two of them should sit down together and lay out a plan of action that they both agree to. We even suggest that both sign it as if it were a contract, thereby reinforcing the protective barriers which will help to prevent him from falling back into old sinful patterns. The stronger they are, the less likely he will breach them later.

There are certain areas of the sex addict's life that every wife should be involved in. First, she should be in charge of the finances, even if he hasn't had a track record of irresponsibility. Generally speaking, men need money to be involved with pornography. Never underestimate the cunning of a man who wants his sin. Steve used to stash money, a little at a time, waiting for the opportunity to go to a massage parlor or porn shop. Once he got serious about changing, he became much more honest.

The other element that has to be available is time. For those men who have set hours of work at a specific location, this doesn't tend to be too difficult. Others have jobs that give them a lot of freedom (i.e., outside salesmen, truck drivers, repairmen, etc.). Setting priorities is of utmost importance. If your husband has this kind of freedom and continues to struggle, you must ask yourselves if it is really worth it for him to keep that job. However, if, for some reason, there simply is no alternative, then the next best thing you can do is to agree that every night you will look him in the eye and ask him how he did that day. Knowing he will have to face that may help him when he faces temptation. However, this system does not usually work smoothly, because it tends to create friction between spouses.

Another area of the husband's life that the wife should be involved in is his devotional time. This means that you must be absolutely committed to meeting with God daily yourself. One thing that helps get the habit established is a structured Bible study. There are many available. You might consider *The Walk of Repentance*,* which was written by my husband with the sexual addict and the hurting wife in mind. It is a 24-week Bible study. A consistent prayer time should be a part of this daily devotion time as well.

Another thing that the wife should monitor is television watching. We, of course, highly recommend that couples simply get rid of the TV. However, if for some reason you are unwilling to do this, at the very least television viewing should be very limited. Pick shows together that you agree would be comparatively "safe." Plan your times to watch the TV, rather than simply turning it on every night and allowing it to rule your home. You must set rules and stick to them.

Another biggie is the Internet! Does your husband have access to the Internet at home or at his workplace? If so, find out if he has ever visited porn sites. If you don't need this service, by all means don't bring it into your home. In my opinion the temptation is too great for any man who struggles with sexual sin. However, if you already have service and it is necessary for you to have access, please get a filtering system installed at once.

---

* Steve Gallagher, *The Walk of Repentance*. Available through Pure Life Ministries.

Lastly, you both must commit to being in church at every opportunity. Again, if you are half-hearted about attending church, you can't expect anything more from your husband.

These are all areas that the wife of a sexual addict should be involved with in her husband's life. As I already stated, holding your husband accountable for his sexual sin is better handled by a male friend. The best scenario would be for your husband to come to the Pure Life Ministries Live-in Program—or at least go through the Overcomers-At-Home Program.[†] You both could receive the counseling, encouragement and accountability that you need. One of the benefits of this is that our counselors are in constant communication with each other about the husband and wife. If the husband is confessing things to his counselor that we feel the wife should be aware of, her counselor shares them with her. This can also be accomplished through a good biblical counselor, as well.[‡]

For the couple who, for whatever reason, feels that the wife should be the one to hold him accountable, the following guidelines are appropriate:

When he confesses struggles, don't insist on details. For instance, if one evening he tells you that he struggled with fantasy that day, you don't need to know what it was about specifically. If he tells you that he went to a massage parlor, don't ask what the girl was like. I think you get the picture.

When he does confess his struggles, you can't allow yourself to fall apart emotionally or yell at him or even lay a guilt trip on him. I know this is a lot to ask, but he has to know that he can be candid without being beaten up for it.

---

† See list of Pure Life Ministries programs in the back of this book or visit our website at *purelifeministries.org*.

‡ I recommend you contact the National Association of Nouthetic Counselors (NANC) at 317.337.9100, *nanc.org* or the International Association of Biblical Counselors (IABC) at 303.469.4222, *iabc.net* to find a biblical counselor in your area.

Once he begins to think he will be punished for his honesty, he won't bother to confess his struggles to you anymore.

Not only must you control your feelings—which very few women can do—but you must also show your appreciation for his honesty. Be supportive of his willingness to be vulnerable. Keep in mind how hard it is for a man to admit these things to a woman, especially to his wife. You must do your best not to bring up his past failures. Be a good listener, and do not take the role of merciless interrogator.

I think you can see by these guidelines why we strongly encourage couples to find someone outside the marriage as a source of accountability. Use whichever principles that apply to your situation, Deanna. Do all that you do with compassion and grace. Be as supportive as you can. If he is sincere, one day you will reap the blessings of your efforts to support him. As Galatians 6:9 says, "And let us not lose heart in doing good, for in due time we shall reap if we do not grow weary."

DIVORCE

Dear Theresa,

It was unclear to me whether or not you were expecting me to respond to your letter in which you explained why you were filing for a divorce. Yet, I assume you wanted some feedback.

Divorce...it is an ugly word isn't it? It involves more than simply the legal dissolution of a marital contract. I believe it has eternal consequences because God says that He hates divorce. (Malachi 2:16) Furthermore, Jesus revealed God's heart concerning this issue when He said, "Because of your hardness of heart, Moses permitted you to divorce your wives; but from the beginning it has not been this way." (Matthew 19:9) In other words, divorce was never a part of God's original plan. It is basically the way many people choose to deal with their marital problems.

The divorce rate among Christians is at an all-time high nowadays. For many, getting a divorce seems like the only way to escape an unhappy marriage or to deal with painful circumstances. However, as Christians we are called to have the mind of Christ which means we are to patiently bear others in spite of their faults.

In your letter you justified divorce because your husband has "committed adultery in his heart." I'm sure that you know that when Jesus condoned divorce in Matthew 5:32 that He was referring to those who were in on-going, unrepentant fornication with another person. Although it is true that adultery begins in the heart, your husband's mental struggles hardly fit into this category.

You said you've had to deal with this for five years now, and "can't take it anymore." I could understand wanting a divorce if your husband had been involved in an affair all this time and had been unwilling to repent, but don't you feel like you're giving up too easily?

Theresa, I encourage you to really seek the Lord about this before you proceed any further. Open up your heart to God's will. He will give you the grace to love and bear your husband. If you'll do this, you will find that the long-term benefits will far outweigh the temporary relief of divorce.

LOST RESPECT

Dear Jeri,

I hear the same thing from many women, "I have lost all respect for my husband." I know how that feels because I experienced the same thing.

The loss of respect comes from seeing a loved one continue to do things that we consider to be shameful and degrading. Women tend to look to the husband to be the strong one of the family, the one whom she can depend upon to exercise wise and stable leadership. Most women want to look up to their husbands. This becomes difficult when the husband allows himself to be controlled by some ungodly passion which could potentially destroy his marriage. Such weakness and lack of self-control often provokes a sense of disdain in the wife's heart toward her husband.

However, it should be remembered that this loss of respect is simply a feeling. For a hurting wife it is a negative emotional response to her husband's failures. This can be overwhelming to those women who have endured so much. In no way do I wish to discount it. I know only too well what it is like to deal with.

The fact that it is a feeling is good news, though, because feelings are something within us that can be dealt with and even changed over time. We may or may not be able to have an effect on whether or not someone else sins. Others' actions are, for the most part, outside of the realm of our control. But our own reaction to their sinful behavior is something we can exert some control over.

So then, what is a wife to do? Paul tells wives that they are to "respect" their husbands. The Greek translation of this word is *phobeo*, which comes from the word for fear. The KJV translates it as reverence. How do you have reverence or even respect for a man involved in perversion? What helps us, is that this is a biblical commandment, not a suggestion or even optional for a godly wife. If it were, Paul might have said something like, "Wives, treat your husbands with respect when their actions show they are worthy of it." It is easy to esteem or show honor to someone who is respectable. As a commandment, however, we are told to do it regardless of how we may feel. It is along the same lines of Jesus telling His followers that they are to love their enemies. Nobody has the capability to do this in his or her own strength. The power to love those who hate us can only come from the Holy Spirit.

It is true that your husband has done disgraceful things. But rather than being disrespectful, consider how Jesus feels about him. He loves him and sees him through eyes of love.

As you learn to walk in the Spirit of Christ, your attitude towards your husband will change. You will still observe his failures, but instead of seeing them through the eyes of a critical spirit, you will begin to see them through the eyes of compassion. The whole key, to respecting your husband, is found in being in the Spirit.

How do you deal with these overwhelming feelings in the meantime? Pray for him, treat him with kindness, and support him as best as you can. You will find that feelings follow behavior, which means that as you do your best to treat him as Jesus would treat him, you will find that your feelings of disgust for him will greatly diminish.

Entrust yourself to the Lord, Jeri. Do your best, stay in prayer, and let the Lord strengthen you and fill you with His Holy Spirit.

THE MERCY LIFE

Dear Yolanda,

I t is always such a joy to receive a letter like yours. In it, you said you wanted to know more about "the mercy life" that you have heard Steve refer to in some of his messages, and how you can apply it in your marriage. You confessed that your struggle with this kind of teaching is that it seems contradictory to show mercy to someone so full of sin.

I went through the same struggle myself. To me, it seemed wrong to be kind to someone who stayed in unrepentant sin. I felt I had to punish sin in some way; let the sinner know I didn't approve of his actions. The whole concept of "love the sinner, hate the sin" was foreign to me and went against my nature. It wasn't until much later that I really came to see that it is "the kindness of God (that) leads you to repentance." (Romans 2:4)

People who do not realize their own sinfulness and wickedness cannot comprehend God's mercy. The reason my husband and I embrace this "mercy life" is because we were such sinners. Until you come to terms with what your heart is like, mercy has little or no real value to you. That is the problem so many of the women I deal with experience. They are looking at their husbands' sin rather than examining their own hearts.

Once you see what a sinner you have been in life and how merciful God has been to you, the gratitude that wells up in your heart moves you to do the same mercy to others, which God has done to you. Unfortunately, most Christians are quick to take God's mercy for themselves, but are slow in giving it out to others.

The "mercy life" is simply a true description of what the Christian life is supposed to be. Extending mercy to another is primarily an act of meeting the needs of that person, looking for nothing in return. For someone thirsty, it is water. For the hungry, it is food. For the homeless, it might be food, clothing or shelter. For an unsaved relative, it might mean sharing one's testimony or continuing to hold him up in prayer. For a starving village in Africa, it could mean donating money, food, or even farm implements. For an orphan, it would be a family who would adopt him.

To live the "mercy life" means to allow God to use you to meet the needs of those He puts in your life. This could be formal ministry or simply the daily life of a godly Christian.

In the context of being married to a man who is struggling with sexual sin, what do you think his greatest needs are? How could God use you to meet those needs?

I would say that holding him accountable in a spirit of love would be considered God's mercy to him. Encouraging him when he's down or giving him a strong exhortation when he sluffs off his responsibilities would both be considered merciful, if done in a spirit of compassion.

The greatest thing you can do to help your husband, however, is to intercede for him regularly and continually. What greater thing could you do for Jessie than to bombard heaven on his behalf? Not only will it have a great effect on his life, as it enables God to move on his behalf, but, perhaps more importantly, it will help you to stay in the right spirit toward him. It's hard to be mad at someone who you are pouring your heart out for every day.

I know you are praying for Jessie. I just want to encourage you to keep pressing in to God for Jessie's sake and also for your own. You will find in Him the answer to every problem and the hope for every dream.

LOST LOVE

Dear Diane,

$\mathcal{I}$ disagree with your statement that in God's eyes, your marriage is over because you don't love your husband anymore. That is not the heart of the Lord, Diane.

Believe me, I know what it's like to live with a man when the feelings are gone. It seems as though nothing can restore the love and respect again. There is little or no desire for reconciliation.

You say that you are friendly with him but have lost your romantic feelings for him. It seems that, in your mind, romantic feelings and love are synonymous. Many Christians fall for this lie because this is the concept that is taught to us by the world. In his book, *At the Altar of Sexual Idolatry,* my husband gave the following illustration of this:

> Perhaps the reason Hollywood so readily promotes the adulterer is because it has such a superficial idea about what love is. In the movies, love is a tidal wave of emotion which overtakes a person almost against his or her own will. How many movies are there where the married woman helplessly "falls in love" with another man? She knows it is wrong, but she just cannot seem to help herself. Of course, the husband is always made to appear to be some monster so that everyone cheers when the anguished wife finally gives in to her feelings and commits adultery.*

From the world's perspective, a person's feelings dictate how they are to treat others. However, this is not the case for Christians who have a much higher calling. Jesus laid out the path for His followers when He said:

---

* Steve Gallagher, *At the Altar of Sexual Idolatry.*

But I say to you who hear, love your enemies, do good to those who hate you, bless those who curse you, pray for those who mistreat you…And just as you want people to treat you, treat them in the same way. And if you love those who love you, what credit is that to you? For even sinners love those who love them. (Luke 6:27-32)

Here we are given a clear-cut command from our Savior to love those who don't treat us the way we think we should be treated. But how can Jesus expect us to have warm feelings for those who curse and mistreat us? He doesn't. Although, we can't control our feelings, we can control our words and actions simply by obeying the words of Jesus.

In the great "love chapter" of I Corinthians 13, fifteen actions are laid out that sum up the word love for the believer. The wife may not have romantic feelings toward her husband, but there is nothing to stop her from being kind, humble, patient, or even self-sacrificing with him. Again, to quote Steve:

> The foundation of biblical love is based upon one's behavior, rather than one's feelings. When a man is being kind to his wife, for instance, he is loving her; thus, when he is being unkind to her, he is not loving her. Since love is a behavior which a person can choose to do, his emotions must always be secondary to his conduct. This is why Jesus could command His followers to love their enemies. He did not expect them to have warm and fuzzy feelings when others mistreated them.[†]

Well, I don't want to belabor the issue, but perhaps I can encourage you to do the following homework assignment:

---

† Steve Gallagher, *At the Altar of Sexual Idolatry.*

Make a commitment that for one month you will do everything within your ability to do things God's way. For thirty days you will set aside your feelings, your agenda, and your plans. Consider this to be a project for the Lord. If nothing has changed for you and your husband after this period, then at that time you can reconsider your options. But during this time frame, you are not to even think about divorce.

You must first come to the Lord with the right attitude, willing to allow Him to change your heart. If you just go through the motions and refuse to open your heart up to Him, this project is doomed from the start. Just ask the Lord to help you be willing to do His will.

Second, each morning throughout this month, during your devotional time, spend some time praying over I Corinthians 13:1-8 and Luke 6:27-46. Meditate and pray over each verse. Ask the Lord to make His words real to you. Ask Him to help you to live out those words in your daily life.

During this one-month period, you must commit to living these words towards your husband. No one is expecting you to do this perfectly, but do the best you can, and do it with all of your heart.

Diane, you said in your letter that you were looking for the will of God for your life. I just want to remind you that it is always the will of God for a believer to treat others—even the unlovable—with love. The best way to stay in His will, is to do His will wherever you are. Of course, if you are simply looking for an excuse to leave your marriage, then none of this will be of any interest to you. However, if you really meant what you said about wanting God's will, then this exercise will put you in the mindset of the Lord where you can better hear His voice.

As I conclude this letter, allow me to speculate on the struggle you will have over doing this experiment. Perhaps as you read my suggestion, an unwillingness rose up in your heart. If it is so, the basis of it is fear. Because you have been hurt and have already decided not to make yourself vulnerable to him any longer, the whole idea of giving yourself emotionally to your husband in this way probably struck dread in your heart.

What I want to help you see, Diane, is that you no longer feel love because you no longer want to give love. You have closed your heart to your husband and just want to get on with your life without him. What you may not realize, though, is that whenever you close your heart to another person, you have closed it to God first.

I know you have been hurt and battered emotionally, but the healing you need will never come by running away from painful circumstances; it will come from the Lord as you remain in His Spirit. I'm not trying to beat up on you, sister. I'm trying to steer you away from a disastrous course.

In your mind you may have it all worked out. You will bring "closure" to this ugly chapter in your life and get on with your life with God. You feel that your marriage has been a mistake that you will now fix. What you will eventually discover is that you will face the same kinds of difficulties and conflicts in other future relationships. If you don't learn how to love others unconditionally where you are, you will live a defeated life, never able to please the Lord and obey His command to "love your neighbor as yourself."

Humble yourself to the Lord, Diane, and allow Him to replace your thoughts with His thoughts and give you a new heart. Then, you will find joy and peace to see you through.

UNTRUSTWORTHY WITH MONEY

Dear Carla,

I don't blame you for feeling as though you can't trust your husband. According to your letter, he continually drains the checking account, runs up credit card debt and then lies about it. All I can say is that you are not expected to trust someone who has proven they are untrustworthy.

Dealing with a husband like this can be very discouraging. It can be extremely frustrating for a responsible person to get a credit card statement in the mail, expecting to find with a zero balance, but discover $700.00 worth of charges instead; to have bounced checks come back to you with $20.00 worth of bank charges tacked onto each one of them; or, to go to make the house payment and discover that the account has been emptied.

You didn't mention whether or not your husband has expressed a willingness to change his behavior. If he seems to be sorrowful over his past actions and is willing to cooperate with you, then there are definite steps you can take to help curb his irresponsible actions.

You might want to seek the aid of a Christian financial advisor. The right person could be a real help to your husband with managing his money. Perhaps a consumer credit agency could assist you in consolidating your debts and set up a reasonable payment plan.

If this isn't possible, then I suggest you do the following: First, sit down with your husband and put a game plan on paper. Once you have completed it, have him sign it, signifying his willingness to cooperate with your plan.

Second, you must either cut up your credit card or, at the very least, put it where he cannot get to it. Just keep in mind that if he knows the credit card number, he can still use it. Don't ever underestimate the craftiness of a man who wants his sin.

Finally, you must take complete control of the checking account. I would even suggest that you have his name taken off it, at least until he has reached a reasonable level of trustworthiness. This will deter him from draining your account on his selfish indulgences. I also suggest that you take steps to ensure that you are the only one to pick up his paycheck. He can either arrange for it to be sent to the house or just tell his boss that you are the only one to pick it up. Obviously, you need to get his ATM card from him, as well. Every morning you can issue him the amount of cash he should need to get through the day.

One of the reasons Steve was able to defeat the power of sexual addiction was that he was so willing to comply with the safeguards I implemented around his life. He knew he couldn't be trusted; so he gladly allowed me to control and manage the money and was accountable to me for his time. Those boundaries kept him from doing something he would later regret in those times of weakness and temptation.

Men bent on having their own way are impossible to help. You cannot monitor someone who is determined to have his sin. If this proves to be your husband's attitude, then you might have to consider taking stronger measures.

I know that he has always been the one to manage the finances, but you can do this, Carla. Turn to the Lord for His help, commit this into His hands and don't be afraid to be strong. Your husband needs your strength right now.

HIGH EXPECTATIONS

Dear Gloria,

Let me start by offering you words of warning: if you don't start being more compassionate and merciful to your husband, you are going to drive him right out the front door.

I guess that statement is an attention grabber! Please, don't take me wrong. My impression of you is that you are very intolerant of sin in both your own life as well as your husband's. In a sense, it is rather admirable for you to take such a stance, but you need to be extremely careful that you don't allow yourself to become self-righteous. If you give over to such an attitude, pretty soon you will be boasting along with the Pharisee, "God, I thank Thee that I am not like other people: swindlers, unjust, adulterers, or even like this tax-gatherer…" (Luke 18:11) You will find your husband beating his chest in humble repentance, while you go home unjustified.

I realize that your strong determination has helped you to overcome problems in your own life. However, not everyone progresses at the same rate and in the same way. You cannot lay down the ultimatum to your husband that "he better be completely healed in three months or it's over." That's unreasonable and rather unmerciful considering how much your husband will have to battle through.

This statement reveals a number of misconceptions about what God is like and what He expects from His followers. First of all, He doesn't put those kinds of time limits on us. He knows how strong the hold sin can have on a person. The Bible says that God is longsuffering with our sin. That doesn't mean that He condones it. It means that He has so much love for the sinner that He is willing to endure with the person's acts of disobedience, as He is breaking the stronghold of those sins in his life.

God isn't intolerant of us, nor is He impatient with us when we're struggling. He loves us deeply and is willing to go to any lengths to discipline us for holiness. He is the surgeon of souls and goes inside our hearts to remove the cancer that would otherwise kill us.

People who demand holiness from others usually have very little comprehension of what true holiness really means. God doesn't live by some rigid set of rules that He never transgresses, therefore He is "perfect." The rules of the Bible stem from God's heart for the rights of people, and His desire that we, too, walk in His love toward others.

Take the last six of the Ten Commandments, for instance. Each of these "rules" have to do with the way we treat other people. God doesn't ask us to keep these rules so we will be rigid Pharisees. He asks us to keep them out of a heart-felt love and devotion for those other people.

I agree with you that your husband is being unloving toward the women he lusts over. While this is true, God is the only one who can help him to overcome that lust. Even if you were somehow able to police him into maintaining a lust-free life, most likely it would only mean that he would become like the Pharisees. They kept the laws of God, to look religious and receive the praise of men, not because they were so filled with love for others that they didn't want to offend them. Lust is something your husband should struggle against, but ultimately it will be the love of God that uproots and supplants it.

If you are living a consecrated life, as you have claimed in your letter, that is wonderful! That consecration should be helping you be more like God, to see people as He sees them, to feel compassion over them as He does and to endure with their failures.

I think you should probably re-evaluate your stringent "guidelines and rules." I know that you were instructed by your counselors to set boundaries for your husband, but I have a feeling that you have gone a little overboard. How can you set a boundary on the mind of another human being? I think it is rather commendable that your husband has been so honest with you, considering how explosive you can be. Your intolerance toward his struggles has probably made him regret he ever opened up to you.

Why not humble yourself, and go to him? Let him know that you were wrong in giving him an ultimatum and that you are going to support him through his struggles. This would mean a lot to him. You would do far more to help him overcome, than if you were to legislate rules into his life he simply is not able to keep. May God bless you in your passion for holiness and your devotion to your husband and those around you.

WATCHING PORNOGRAPHY

Dear Wanda,

*W*ithout being condescending, I agree with your statement that you are very confused. I suspect this is exactly what your husband has been hoping for. Confusion wears down one's resistance to evil. The primary question of your letter was: "Is it wrong to view pornography with my husband in the privacy of our home?" In our "anything goes" society, most think that there is nothing at all wrong with it. But I assume you are looking for a biblical response from someone who has been there and done that.

Many years ago I was, like you, so confused and hurt. At the time, pornography seemed to be the only way to bring Steve and me together after I had tried everything else to keep him from being unfaithful to me. His arguments that it was something we could enjoy together and at the same time satisfy his obsession and end any further sneaking around, were very persuasive. I had no inkling then how untrue his arguments were. I paid a heavy price spiritually and emotionally.

Initially things went well. Steve was so grateful that he wouldn't have to sneak around anymore. In his sin-sick mind, I think he sincerely believed what he told me. At the beginning of this period, he treated me better than he had in years. But before long, the thrill of it began to dissipate—as sin always does—and he began sneaking out to massage parlors again. Then Steve suggested that we invite other people into our sex life. Again, in my obsessive desire to keep him, I reluctantly agreed. We both began to spiral downward. After just a few months of it, I became numb to this new fetish as well. My conscience was being seared. My sense of moral conviction was almost on empty. It was then that I finally realized I would have to leave him. My swinging days were over—I wanted out of a marriage gone sour.

Had I only known what it would cost me, I never would

have gotten involved in the first place. In my great determination to win my husband's love, no matter what, I was willing to sacrifice my self-respect, the morals I was raised with, and most importantly, my walk with God. For years, I was riddled with guilt and shame over the things I had seen and participated in just to keep my husband.

But that wasn't all. It took years for those images and unpleasant memories to go away. For some time, I had to deal with unnatural desires I had never experienced before. Pornographic movies create the illusion that everybody is highly sexed and perverted. They warp a person's perspectives of other people. For a long time, I saw every woman as someone who wanted to seduce my husband and every man as a pervert.

Having said all this, allow me to ask you some penetrating questions. Do you think it is right to be so given over to a man that you would consider degrading yourself with pornography just to keep the relationship together? What kind of a person will you have to become to keep him happy? Are you really willing to involve yourself with and consent to your husband's secret perversions? Do you realize that becoming involved with pornography will only give your husband the license to openly lust over girls in your presence? Are you sure you are willing to subject yourself to that? Are you willing to involve yourself with something as evil and dark as pornography? Are you willing to walk away from God for the sake of appeasing your husband? Once you have hardened your heart against the Lord and filled your mind with perversion, what is going to stop you from taking the next step and the one after that? These are questions you better carefully consider before venturing an inch further.

I believe your letter to me was a sincere plea for help just as someone who would cry out trapped under a pile of rubble. Pray for God's strength, put your foot down, and tell your husband you not only disapprove of but are unwilling to become involved with his perversion.

THE IMPORTANCE OF GRATITUDE

Dear Sylvia,

You wanted me to remind you again of why you should be grateful. Bless your heart. I gather from your letter that you are struggling with an ungrateful and critical spirit. It is so hard to walk this narrow path at times, isn't it? I know I had my days when I just wanted to throw in the towel and say, "Forget it! I'm gonna' be mad and bitter and I'm gonna' enjoy it—so just leave me alone!" It reminds me of a bad hair day. You get so frustrated, all you want to do is shave your head bald! Of course, you don't do it because you know tomorrow it will be better.

But there is a life that can be lived that is so much higher than a white-knuckle existence, hoping that one day God will notice you and respond to your prayers. You must first count your blessings and acknowledge that God has truly been better to you than you deserve—that goes for all of us.

I have heard it said that a grateful heart is a full heart, and I have found it to be true. In fact, I would go so far as to say that the main reason for my present joy and my husband's victory over sexual sin is directly related to our level of gratitude. Had we never opened our eyes to see God's merciful dealings in our lives we would be full of misery, regret, and defeat.

Please understand that you must choose to be grateful—it is something you do. Instead of allowing yourself to gripe and complain about all of the things in life that aren't right, you have to make the decision to declare all of the wonderful things that God has done for you. And guess what? You can't allow your feelings to dictate when you will be grateful. It is easier to see the negative and to believe the worst, but if you will make a willful choice to see God in the light of His goodness, your attitude will change despite your circumstances. Being thankful keeps you in the same Spirit Jesus lived in while on earth. The more you express gratitude in your heart, the more grateful you become. You begin to see how merciful God has been to you throughout your life—even when you were His enemy.

What Paul taught is very true: You reap what you sow. If you cultivate a thankful heart, you will reap the joy and contentment that comes with it. Likewise, if you give over to a bitter and pessimistic spirit, you will reap an abundant harvest of misery. This misery, in turn, will affect every aspect of your life, especially your loved ones.

At the Pure Life Ministries Live-in program, a regular homework assignment for men full of self-pity or resentment is to write out a gratitude list of fifty things they are grateful for about the person or situation they have been grumbling about. This can be quite a challenge for those who are so accustomed to dwelling on negativity. But it is phenomenal how quickly a sincere person's outlook on life or a particular circumstance can change from such a simple assignment.

What keeps us defeated and in an ungrateful spirit is a lack of faith. Once you begin to see what the Lord is really like and how intimately involved He is in your life, you just want to sit down and thank Him for all that He has done for you.

There is so much to be thankful for. I could write an entire book on the subject. Just on a spiritual level, we can thank the Father for sending His Son. We can thank Jesus for leaving His throne, coming to this earth and dying on the cross for our sins. We can thank the Holy Spirit for carefully arranging the circumstances of our lives in order that we would see our need for God, convicting us of our sins at just the right time and leading us to the right church or person who helped us find the Lord.

We should also regularly thank God for all that He

gives—for free! Such as? God gives us the keys to the kingdom (Matthew 16:19), the power to tread upon serpents (Luke 10:19), peace (John 14:27), eternal life (Romans 6:23), all things pertaining to life and godliness (II Peter 1:3-4), spiritual gifts (I Corinthians 12), knowledge of the mysteries of heaven (Matthew 13:11), power to become the sons of God (John 1:12), and the list goes on and on. Considering all these things, it is possible for a person to live in a spirit of gratitude all the time.

In your case, Sylvia, I encourage you to spend some time meditating upon all of the good God is doing for you through this difficult situation. Make out your own list. Just to give you a few examples: He is there as a refuge for you; He is trying to do good for you and your husband; He is showing both of you how much you need Him; He is deepening your faith, etc.

I can't say it enough: there is so much to be thankful for! One of the things we tell the men at the live-in program is that for everything we can see that the Lord has done for us, there are a hundred other things that we don't even know about. It is so important to cultivate a grateful heart, because it helps a person put things in proper perspective.

God has nothing but good for you, Sylvia. Wouldn't it be better to express your gratitude to Him regularly for His kindness than to be a habitual complainer? You can choose to be grateful! God is for you and will grant you the grace to endure and bring you through deep waters.

DON'T STOP BELIEVING

Dear Marcie,

I can hear the pain in your letter. Your remark, "He doesn't love me or the babies at all; he's just consumed with himself," says it all. And that is the hallmark of sexual sin, isn't it? Total self-absorption. Having someone empathize with you may help a little, but it doesn't change your husband.

I think your approach is very good and healthy. You do have to get on with your life in God, Marcie. It isn't as though you haven't been patient with Wayne.

Although, you may not be able to return to the mission field, there are plenty of things you can do to occupy your life with other people's needs. By helping others you, in turn, will be blessed and will receive healing yourself.

Continue to pray and believe God to draw Wayne. With God, ALL things are possible. Don't give in to discouragement and unbelief. Don't look at Wayne, or you will grow even more discouraged and you will give up. But look to the One who can change him.

It takes sin like this in some lives to bring them to the place of total and absolute surrender. I know, in my husband's life, he purposed in his heart early on to be as committed to the Lord as he had been to sexual sin. It had to be that way for him. Nothing short of an all-out consecration would keep him living in victory. And God is making it so in Wayne's life. Men, like our husbands, can't straddle the fence—one foot in and one foot out. Sin will always win in the face of compromise and a half-hearted commitment.

We have seen the most hopeless sinners, the most vile offenders, come to God when everyone else had given up on them. My husband was one of these untouchables.

Hang in there, Marcie. Go after God with all you have. Pursue a holy life, raise your children for the Lord, and don't stop believing in the power of God to set your husband free.

THE ENABLER WIFE

Dear Robin,

I'm so sorry to hear you just received the awful revelation
that your husband has been having numerous affairs over
the entire nineteen years of your marriage. In your letter, you
made some comments that help me get a better idea of why
Jake was able to live this double life for so long.

You mentioned that there were many instances over the
years that you should have realized what was going on. You
said, "I guess I just wanted to believe what my husband was
telling me."

That statement perfectly epitomizes what we have coined
as "The Enabler Wife." Many women simply don't feel as
though they can handle the fact that their husbands are being
unfaithful to them. The thought of infidelity is so painful and
overwhelming that they simply shut it out of their minds. It is
easier for them to stifle their suspicions rather than to have to
deal with them head-on.

Let's face it, when a woman discovers that her husband
has had numerous extramarital affairs there are no easy
solutions. For one thing she is devastated. So, of course,
sticking her head in the sand, pretending that there is no
adultery helps to escape that pain. Deep down inside, the
hurting wife knows that she will have to make some very
painful decisions. But many women are simply too dependent
upon their husbands to even consider leaving them. Others
are too weak to confront their husbands. The easiest recourse
is to simply act as though there isn't a problem and hope that
it will resolve itself or fizzle out over time.

The unfortunate consequence to this kind of reaction
is that nothing ever happens to force the husband to make
a decision about his sin. His wife's lack of response allows
him to keep his home *and* his mistresses: every adulterer's

dream. Since his wife won't confront him and doesn't force him to decide between her and his sin, he is able to keep them both. In the meantime, he is lost and on his way to hell. That's a high price to pay for the easy route, and it exposes the selfishness in this woman's heart to leave him in such a predicament, for the sake of maintaining her image and comfort zone

I'm so glad to hear that you were able to confront Jake when you received the undeniable evidence of his affairs. I'm sure you would agree that finally dealing with it has been a tremendous weight lifted off your back. And look at Jake! He's on fire for God! He's been stuck in his sin for so many years—going to church but just as lost as he could be. Now he, too, is free! All because you made him decide between you and his sin. It doesn't always end so happily, but it sure is a blessing when it does.

Thank you for sharing this victory with me, Robin. I hope to hear more wonderful testimonies again in the future.

SEPARATED WITH A BOYFRIEND

Dear Lisa,

I will get right to the point and try to answer your questions. It seems to me that having a boyfriend will not only make the two-year separation from your husband worse, but it will negatively impact every area of your life. I believe you know this deep down in your heart, or you wouldn't have asked about it.

You made it clear that you are not having sex with him, but I don't think you can justify this relationship on that basis—or any other for that matter. In God's eyes, you are still a married woman and should remain devoted to your husband—even if he is being unfaithful. Your attitude should be that he is the only man on this earth. Yes, it is true, he is off in sin and showing no remorse or willingness to repent. Perhaps, if you feel the Lord releasing you from this marriage, you should consider divorce. But for right now, you must continue to act like a married woman—this is pleasing to the Lord.

It seems to me that you are attempting to fill the empty place in your heart with this boyfriend. You are looking to him to meet your emotional needs, rather than to the Lord. One of the problems with this is that you are not receiving the emotional and spiritual healing the Lord wants to give you. By doing things your way, you are keeping the sores open which is making your condition worse and worse.

I know how painful it is to go through this experience, but if you don't turn to the Comforter while in the fire, it is all for nought. The Lord is trying to do a deep, eternal work in your heart through your trials, but this will only happen as you learn to turn to Him in your pain rather than to another man. Not only that, but as you trust the Lord with your life through this situation, He will bless you and help you. Don't tie His hands, Lisa.

Having a boyfriend also produces its own problems, further complicating matters. What kind of message is this sending your children? How does it look to others who are looking at you as a representative of Christ? What is going to happen to him if and when your husband repents? Will you just dump him, once you no longer need his companionship? Or, will you go against God's restoration of your marriage by refusing to reunite with your husband? Also, how does being involved with a married woman affect this man's walk with the Lord? Please stop and consider what you are doing. Don't allow your own desires to cloud your thinking and continue to move outside of God's will.

Instead of looking to some guy for fulfillment or to escape your problems, why not make Jesus your boyfriend? Spend your time with Him, talk to Him, be with Him. Only He can fill your needs and bless your life.

LETTER FROM A HUSBAND

Dear Valerie,

I am really stepping out on a limb, writing this letter. This is something I would normally never do, but I felt led of the Lord to follow up on a letter I received from your husband. In it, he expressed his frustration over your lack of concern about his sexual sin.

I respect John's sincere desire to get total victory over his addiction. He seems to be willing to do whatever it takes to break free. He takes his sin seriously and wants it out of his life. It is obvious in his letter that he desperately desires that you come to grips with what is going on and try to be more supportive.

One of the things he said was that you "live in a fairy-tale world, and believe that everything will just work itself out, somehow." I have included a letter to a lady named Robin* that I would encourage you to read. She, too, struggled with not wanting to face the reality of her husband's sin.

Another thing that John mentioned was that he was under "a tremendous temptation to give up." That statement raised a major red flag to me, Valerie. This lets me know that he is growing weary and is starting to lose hope. This sense was further reinforced when he said that "it is very disheartening to go this thing alone."

Valerie, John is your husband, and his problem is your problem; likewise, his challenge becomes your challenge. I don't believe he wants you to panic or go into a depression over it, but your refusal to deal with reality concerning this issue forces him to fend for himself. Remember: you two are one flesh.

Pornography addiction is very real and extremely powerful. I think it would be good for you to read my

* See the Enabler Wife, page 144.

husband's book, *At the Altar of Sexual Idolatry*. It not only describes the addiction, but the consequences of it and how it affects others beside the addict. I think reading this book will help you to see the enormous battle your husband is facing.

I want to encourage you to really begin interceding for John. Start asking him how he is doing. Begin to take an active part in the process of overcoming this sin. I feel that your husband will start to win this battle with your encouragement, support, and prayers. I trust this letter will help to motivate you toward the right direction—alongside your husband.

DEALING WITH UNFORGIVENESS

Dear Rita,

I appreciate your seeking advice as to how to forgive someone who's hurt you so deeply. You said that people have accused you of being unforgiving because you still struggle with certain feelings directly related to your husband's infidelity. Let me tell you Rita, as well-intentioned as some people may be, many of them do not understand the depth of your pain. They have no idea how devastating your husband's struggle with sexual sin has been to you. It is not necessarily unforgiveness you are struggling with. You are just human and are still working through some very serious issues.

You seem to be a very sincere Christian woman who desires to please the Lord. In your letter, you did not come across vindictive at all. Your statement, "I want to be healed, and I want my husband healed so that we can be pleasing to the Lord together," doesn't sound like a woman full of bitterness.

So on that basis, I will address your question. Jesus dealt less with the outward and more with people's hearts. With precision, He went right to the root issue buried deep within. Like a two-edged sword, His words pierced through dividing the soul and spirit, judging the thoughts and intents of the heart. In Matthew 5, when He talked about heart adultery, He was not giving wives license to divorce their husbands. He was showing lust-filled men the depravity of their hearts. It was the same thing with anger. He said that if you are angry at someone, you are in the exact same spirit as a murderer. The words of Jesus expose our hearts and reveal what hypocrites we can be. We judge according to outward appearances, but God looks upon the heart.

Forgiveness is the same. I realize you are struggling with feelings of betrayal and bitterness. Who wouldn't, considering

what you've had to endure? You are right now in the process
of fighting through some very painful issues that have been
devastating. Please understand that feelings come and go, but
the Lord is more concerned with what is occurring in your
heart. From what you expressed in your letter, it seems to
me that you are simply wanting the best for your husband.
Yes, you have those times of anger, but for the most part you
sincerely desire to see him get free. You love him and want
him to make it. You don't bring up the past and throw it in his
face.

Forgiveness is a process that takes time. I don't mean to
imply that we are excused for ever being unforgiving. What
I mean is that it takes time for the wife to feel like she can
trust her husband again. Because he is the one who broke
that trust, the burden is on his shoulders to re-establish a
relationship built upon trust and truthfulness.

The forgiving wife wants her husband to make it, does
everything she can to encourage him, and therefore expects
him to take the situation seriously. A wife who is unforgiving,
on the other hand, continually reminds him of his past
offenses and anticipates his constant failure. This of course,
only serves to further demoralize him and retard his efforts to
get free. The idol in the heart of an unforgiving wife is s-e-l-f.
She is far more concerned about protecting herself from ever
being hurt again, than she is about restoring her marriage or
supporting her husband in his struggle to overcome sexual
sin.

Don't be too hard on yourself, Rita. It seems that the two
of you are well on your way to putting this whole, ugly affair
behind you. God will help you get through it. The feelings
of anger will subside, and your heart will open up to your
husband once again.

FEELING BETRAYED

Dear Rebecca,

I can't tell you how many times I have heard the words "I feel so betrayed" from hurting wives whose husbands have been unfaithful. Betrayal is only a vague concept until you actually experience the sting of it personally. It leaves you feeling totally abandoned and empty. The following are some definitions and synonyms of the word abandon: to cast off, discard, drop, scrap, reject, run out on, or turn one's back on. I'm sure you can relate to each one of these descriptions.

I suspect if your husband were to read this letter, he would say that he didn't intentionally do any of those things to you. It isn't that he was unfaithful to you because he had some desire to hurt you; he was unfaithful because he was driven by a selfish lust for sex. His offense against you, of course, was a blatant disregard for your feelings but was unlikely a premeditated desire to hurt you.

Nevertheless, a man cannot cut any deeper into a woman's heart than to take what is so personal and give it away to someone else. Sexual intimacy between a married couple is the greatest expression of their love for each other.

I can remember so well the intense pain I experienced dealing with Steve's unfaithfulness. To me our intimacy was sacred. Saying "I do" at the altar made it exclusive and therefore off-limits to others. He was mine and I was his. What we had together in private was ours, and I was the only one who should know him in that way. Marital sex is the tie that physically binds two individuals together and its sanctity is due to the spiritual union that is created.

When I found out that Steve was being unfaithful, I was crushed. He was spiritually becoming "one flesh" with anything with a skirt, giving away what was MINE! Our circle of unity had been broken—our marriage bed defiled.

We no longer had that special oneness which belonged only to us. Our sexual intimacy had been cheapened—actually nullified—because it was shared with many others. It had little or no value to him because he preferred a cheap thrill rather than the real thing: me, his wife. The pleasure he wanted from our union could be found or purchased on any street corner or in any massage parlor.

As far as I was concerned there was now nothing left that was ours as a married couple. We were just two people living together, sharing space. It killed me. Day after day the pain of the reality that our marriage was gone swept over me like sea billows. While it was unbearable to me at times, he seemed to be completely unmoved by the devastation and misery he was causing us.

And yet, Rebecca, somehow in the midst of the overwhelming grief, Jesus came in. Although the pain didn't go away, it did somehow magnify the greatness of the love of God toward me. So then the very thing that I thought would destroy me, became the means by which God would extend to me an abundant life in Him in the heat of an intense battle.

I am grateful, so very grateful, that God spared no expense to give me more of what I needed: Jesus. He used the hurt, the pain, the misery—all of it—to bring this about.

Your feelings of betrayal are real, but there is life—abundant life—to be found in the ashes. You have hope, not just because you have a husband who is now repenting, but because you have a Savior who wishes to flood your soul with His wonderful, life-giving Spirit. My prayer for you is that one day you, too, will have a marriage that is deeper and stronger than it would have been, had there been no betrayal at all.

BIZARRE SEX

Dear Elizabeth,

our letter was brief and to the point, and yet I sensed a much bigger question than just, "Is oral sex wrong?" This gave me the impression that your husband is asking you to do all kinds of things you consider abnormal. It seemed to me that your question about oral sex was the only way you were able to sum this all up in your letter.

I don't feel that anybody can answer that question for you, but that it is something you must take to the Lord. However, please allow me to make a few comments now.

First, many ministers would point to Paul's reference to lesbianism in Romans 1 where he condemns their "exchang(ing) the natural function for that which is unnatural" to show that oral sex is a form of perversion and therefore sinful. They are possibly right.

Second, anything out of the ordinary could very well be a dangerous stumblingblock for a man who has been involved in sexual perversion most of his life. Especially disturbing is how conducive oral sex can be to sexual fantasy.

Having expressed these things, let me say something about marital sex. God intended intimacy between the husband and wife to be satisfying, pleasurable, and yes, even thrilling! We needn't be all sanctimonious about it. It is our Heavenly Father's desire to see married couples enjoy each other's bodies. Selflessly giving pleasure to the other person could arguably be considered the greatest act of love, provided, of course, that both partners are in this same mindset.

Ultimately, Steve and I have concluded that Paul's words in Romans 14 were appropriate words of advice (even though oral sex wasn't the context): "I know and am convinced in the Lord Jesus that nothing is unclean in itself; but to him who thinks anything to be unclean, to him it is unclean."

Elizabeth, what I would suggest to you is to make a list of everything your husband desires of you in bed. Point by point go down that list prayerfully, and try to hear the voice of the Lord. Is this something that is filthy? Is it something that would encourage my husband's warped perspectives of sexuality? Is it something that would be displeasing to God? Or is this something that could be considered a way of blessing the other person without displeasing the Lord? The balance you need is to have freedom and pleasure in your intimacy without it leading to perversion or self-condemnation. I hope this will prove to be helpful.

FAIRY-TALE MARRIAGE

Dear Heather,

The way you described in your letter what marriage should be like sounds wonderful! What woman wouldn't desire all of those attributes in a husband? Unfortunately, Heather, I think you are setting yourself up for a real let down. What will you do when you come to the realization that your husband can't live up to your expectations? You've only been married for three months, and you are already beginning to see that Will is human, with shortcomings just like everyone else.

In your letter, you expressed that he "should be there to meet your emotional needs," "be kind and considerate," "think about what you want, without having to be told," and so on. One of the things that brought you into the reality that your husband was less than perfect was when you began to notice that he had roving eyes for other women, when, in your words, "he should only have eyes for me." You shouldn't panic, Heather, but you do need to be more realistic and a little less selfish in your expectations.

There's nothing wrong with wanting your husband to think of you as the only woman on earth or to treat you like his queen. God desires that for your marriage, as well. You must come to grips with the fact that the road you must travel to arrive at that place is neither quick nor easy.

I found it interesting that in your letter you didn't once mention your desire to be a blessing to your husband. The whole letter was about how you wanted him to make *you* happy, and the confusion you are now experiencing in his failure to do so.

I can remember, only too well, how I felt just as bewildered when I first got married. I, too, was very selfish in my approach to marriage. I expected Steve to meet my every emotional need, to fulfill my every longing, etc. You can imagine my frustration and disillusionment when he did just exactly the opposite of what I expected. Before long I was so discontent and miserable.

It took time, but gradually I began to realize that marriage was not about *me*, it was about the other person—my husband! With the Lord's consistent prodding, I began to really put my heart into my marriage. As I sincerely sought to bless him (rather than looking for a blessing for myself), I began to find a wonderful place of joy and contentment. And the more I did for Steve, the more he did for me and vice-versa. As each of us received kindness from the other, we were motivated to reciprocate in the same spirit.

Now, I can honestly say I have a husband like the one you described in your letter, but this didn't come cheaply or immediately. It took time and much hard work. Heather, instead of thinking about how you want your husband to treat you, spend some time contemplating the qualities of a good wife. Perhaps you should make a list as to all of the things you think a woman should be and do for her husband. Start by praying over Proverbs 31 which gives a portrait of a virtuous woman. As you do, the words of Jesus will mean so much more: "Therefore, however you want people to treat you, so treat them, for this is the Law and the Prophets." (Matthew 7:12)

ENGAGED TO A PORN ADDICT

Dear Alissa,

I am responding to your letter requesting advice about your engagement with Mark. You shared that one of the things that attracted you to him was his active involvement in the worship team at your church. However, you lost a great deal of your respect and trust for him when—unbeknownst to him—you ran across pornographic materials on his computer yesterday. Now you are questioning your decision to marry him.

Alissa, as his fiancé, you have the right to ask Mark if he ever struggles with sexual sin. If he acknowledges his problem, you can move forward with the assurance that he is willing to be honest with you. A lack of truthfulness about it will tell you that he would rather lie than deal with his problems in a forthright manner.

You should insist that he confess his sin to the pastor. This is especially important since he has such a visible position in the church. The apostle John said, "If we say that we have fellowship with Him and yet walk in the darkness, we lie and do not practice the truth." (I John 1:6) Mark will never get free as long as he keeps his sin secret.

If he is unwilling to acknowledge his pornography addiction to your pastor, I would put this relationship "on hold" until he gets serious about overcoming it. A lack of honesty with you and his spiritual leaders should be a major red flag to you and is an indicator about what you could expect in your marriage. If he will not deal with this issue now, then you can bet he won't take it seriously once he has you locked into a marriage.

If he *is* willing to come clean, then you should watch his spiritual progress with caution. I will warn you that being married to a sexual addict will be nothing but heartache and misery for you. Please proceed very cautiously.

30 DAY *Journal*

"The LORD is near to the
brokenhearted, And saves those who
are crushed in spirit. Many are the afflictions
of the righteous; But the LORD delivers
him out of them all." Psalms 34:18-19

"Love reveals itself to love.
We must apprehend Him by affection."
Anonymous

"More than that, I count all things
to be loss in view of the surpassing value
of knowing Christ Jesus my Lord, for whom
I have suffered the loss of all things, and
count them but rubbish in order that
I may gain Christ." Philippians 3:8

"Measure thy life by loss and not
by gain, not by the wine drunk but by the
wine poured forth, for love's strength standeth
in love's sacrifice and he who has suffered
most has most to give." Jonathan Goforth

"For the whole Law is fulfilled in
one word, in the statement, 'You shall love
your neighbor as yourself.'"
Galatians 5:14

"For he will deliver the needy when he
cries for help, the afflicted also, and him
who has no helper. He will have compassion
on the poor and needy, and the lives
of the needy he will save."

Psalm 72:12-13

"A man should settle himself
so fully in God, that he need not to seek
many comforts of men."
Gerhard Groote

"Blessed is a man who perseveres under
trial; for once he has been approved, he will
receive the crown of life, which the Lord has
promised to those who love Him."
James 1:12

"If I find in myself a desire which no experience in this world can satisfy, the most probable explanation is that I was made for another world." C.S. Lewis

"Be strong, and let your heart take
courage, all you who hope in the LORD."
Psalm 31:24

"We would willingly have others
perfect, and yet we amend not our
own faults. And thus it appeareth, how
seldom we weigh our neighbor in the
same balance with ourselves."
Gerhard Groote

"In the same way, you wives,
be submissive to your own husbands so
that even if any of them are disobedient to the
word, they may be won without a word by the
behavior of their wives, as they observe your
chaste and respectful behavior." I Peter 3:1-2

"Sometimes it feels like God has chained us to sorrow and the chains are too heavy to move. But what He is after is the heart cry in the midst of the worst trials: 'The Lord's lovingkindnesses indeed never cease, for His compassions never fail…'" Anonymous

"Behold, the eye of the LORD
is on those who fear Him, on those
who hope for His lovingkindness."
Psalm 33:18

"If I think that faith means to gain
a favorable ending to what I am in faith for,
that is not faith. Faith believes God no matter
what the outcome is; satisfaction with the will
of God, no matter what it means is faith."

Anonymous

"'The LORD is my portion,' says my
soul, 'Therefore I have hope in Him.'
The LORD is good to those who wait
for Him, to the person who seeks Him."
Lamentations 3:24-25

"When a man cometh to that estate that
he seeketh not his comfort from any creature,
then doth he begin to perfectly relish God,
then shall he be contented with whatsoever
doth befall him." Anonymous

"For if He causes grief, then He will
have compassion according to His abundant
lovingkindness. For He does not afflict
willingly, or grieve the sons of men."
Lamentations 3:32-33

"Put me like a seal over your heart, like
a seal on your arm. For love is as strong
as death, jealousy is as severe as Sheol; its
flashes are flashes of fire, the very flame of
the LORD. Many waters cannot quench love,
nor will rivers overflow it." Song of Songs 8:6-7

"For some years now it has been my
abiding conviction that it is impossible to
enjoy true happiness without being entirely
devoted (surrendered) to God."
David Brainerd

"Though the fig tree should not
blossom, and there be no fruit on the
vines… and there be no cattle in the stalls, yet
I will exult in the LORD, I will rejoice in the
God of my salvation." Habakkuk 3:17-18

"I love the LORD, because He hears
my voice and my supplications. Because
He has inclined His ear to me, therefore
I shall call upon Him as long as I live."
Psalm 116:1-2

"Little children guard yourselves from idols."
I John 5:21

"For it is God who is at work in you,
both to will and to work for His good
pleasure. Do all things without grumbling
or disputing; that you may prove yourselves
to be blameless and innocent children of God
above reproach…" Philippians 2:13-15

"We are the broken, You are the Healer;
Jesus Redeemer, mighty to save."

"Sin is the disease of the soul.
Holiness is health to the soul. If you are
healthy in your soul, your emotions and mind
will become holy." J. B. Chapman

"Why are you in despair, O my soul?
And why have you become disturbed within
me? Hope in God, for I shall again praise Him
for the help of His presence."
Psalm 42:5

"Kindness indeed, that eternal life should
come to visit mortals, and to procure eternal
life for them, and then confer it on them!"
Adam Clarke

"Truly, Truly I say to you, unless a grain of
wheat fall into the earth and dies, it remains by
itself alone; but if it dies it bears much fruit."
John 12:24

"Someday you will understand that it was
all just Jesus, and then you will understand."
Martha Wing Robinson

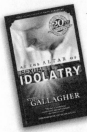

NEW! *From* ASHES *to* BEAUTY

SPIRITUAL TRUTHS FOR REBUILDING & REVITALIZING YOUR MARRIAGE

THERE IS HOPE FOR EVERY MARRIAGE...
Even in the aftermath of sexual sin.

Jeff Colón's marriage stands as a testimony of God's power to restore any marriage, even one that has been ravaged by sexual sin and drug addiction. Christian marriages are under attack as never before. Couples are suffering more than ever under the same despair that once gripped Jeff and his wife, Rose – Is there really hope for my marriage?

THE ANSWER IS A RESOUNDING YES! ...but the solution wasn't the typical fare found in Christian marriage books. Jeff and Rose had to go to the heart of the problem... they needed something more than outward alterations; they needed an inner transformation. Jeff's personal journey and his experience counseling men and couples qualifies him to share the biblical truths that will restore any marriage *From Ashes to Beauty!*

Includes A Study Guide For Each Chapter

THE WALK SERIES

WHETHER USED INDIVIDUALLY OR COLLECTIVELY, EACH OF THESE BIBLE STUDIES IS A GREAT TOOL FOR PERSONAL GROWTH OR GROUP DISCIPLESHIP.

THE WALK OF REPENTANCE

A 24-week Bible study for the Christian who desires to be more deeply consecrated to God. Experience the times of spiritual refreshing that follow repentance.

A LAMP UNTO MY FEET

A 12-week journey through the beautiful Psalm 119 and the life of David. Every reader will be brought into a deeper love, respect and appreciation for God's Word.

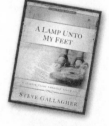

PRESSING ON TOWARD THE HEAVENLY CALLING

The Prison Epistles are a divine archive of profound revelations about the kingdom of God. This 12-week study will challenge you to reach for the abundant life in God that Paul testifies is available to every one of us.

HE LEADS ME BESIDE STILL WATERS

A practical study of the choicest Psalms. This 12-week study takes you right into the intimate interactions between pious men and a loving, caring God and evokes a determined desire to find His Presence for yourself.

Pure Life Ministries

Pure Life Ministries helps Christian men achieve lasting freedom from sexual sin. The Apostle Paul said, "Walk in the Spirit and you will not fulfill the lust of the flesh." Since 1986, Pure Life Ministries (PLM) has been discipling men into the holiness and purity of heart that comes from a Spirit-controlled life. At the root, illicit sexual behavior is sin and must be treated with spiritual remedies. Our counseling programs and teaching materials are rooted in the biblical principles that, when applied to the believer's daily life, will lead him out of bondage and into freedom in Christ.

Biblical Teaching Materials

Pure Life offers a full line of books, audiotapes and videotapes specifically designed to give men the tools they need to live in sexual purity.

Residential Care

The most intense and involved counseling PLM offers comes through the **Live-in Program** (6-12 months), in Dry Ridge, Kentucky. The godly and sober atmosphere on our 45-acre campus provokes the hunger for God and deep repentance that destroys the hold of sin in men's lives.

Help At Home

The **Overcomers At Home Program** (OCAH) is available for those who cannot come to Kentucky for the Live-in program. This twelve-week counseling program features weekly counseling sessions and many of the same teachings offered in the Live-in Program.

Care For Wives

Pure Life Ministries also offers help to wives of men in sexual sin. Our wives' counselors have suffered through the trials and storms of such a discovery and can offer a devastated wife a sympathetic ear and the biblical solutions that worked in their lives.

Pure Life Ministries
14 School St. • Dry Ridge • KY • 41035
Office: 859.824.4444 • Orders: 888.PURE.LIFE
info@purelifeministries.org
www.purelifeministries.org